The Cost of the Anointing

WORKBOOK

Dr. Mia Y. Merritt

Copyright ©2013
by
Mia Y. Merritt, Ed.D

All rights reserved. No part of this book
may be reproduced in any form without permission
in writing from the author or publisher.

ISBN # 978-0-9720398-3-3

Other Books by Mia Y. Merritt:
Prosperity is Your Birthright!
Prosperity is Your Birthright Workbook
Destined for Great Things!
Destined for Great Things Workbook
Words of Inspiration: Golden Nuggets for the Wise at Heart
Road to Inner Joy & Peace
Releasing Emotional Baggage
Money & How it Multiplies
Life After High School
Life After High School Workbook
The Cost of the Anointing

Library of Congress Cataloging
in-Publication Data

Merritt, Mia

First Printing 2013
Printed in the U.S.A.

About this Workbook

Hello my friend,

Before you continue turning the pages of this workbook, make sure that you have read the entire book 'The Cost of the Anointing' because the activities in this workbook are directly correlated to the chapters of the book. The answers are found within the pages of the chapters in the book, so it would be of great benefit to you if you worked in this workbook with the book by your side. If you try to complete this workbook without reading the book first, you are defeating the purpose and your results will not be effective.

If you have completed the book and are ready to embark upon the activities in the workbook, then you must be willing to "BE" the following things:

- prepared to do some writing
- mentally ready to do some thinking
- emotionally stable enough to do some soul-searching
- true to your inner self
- psychologically ready to face your hidden fears and/or demons
- able to confront the things that have hindered you from moving forward in Christ
- ready to identify your spiritual gifts in God
- willing to be elevated to a new level of thinking

This workbook is an interactive, hands-on, thought-provoking guide about YOU! It is designed to help you understand how the anointing is earned through difficulties, but helps you to realize that the reward of having God's anointing upon your life is far better than any test you can endure. This workbook will make you think - and think hard! If you are honest with yourself, healing will take place, but you must be willing to face any hurt, guilt, unforgiveness, anger or bitterness in order to release it. Completing this workbook will enlighten you to recognize things in yourself that you probably hadn't thought about in years. You will become a new person as a result of completing the activities in this workbook!
Are you ready? Are you Set? Then, let's go.

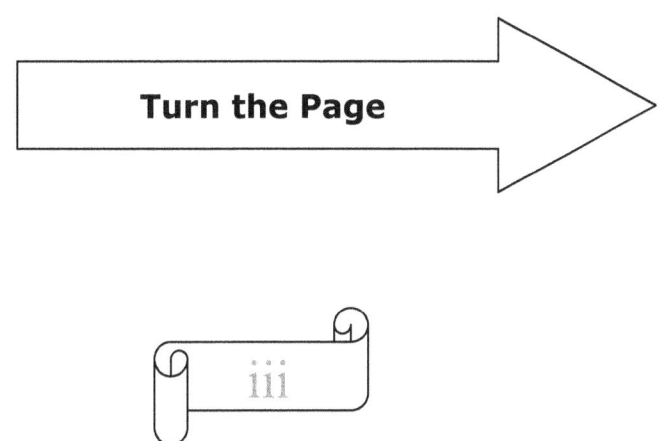

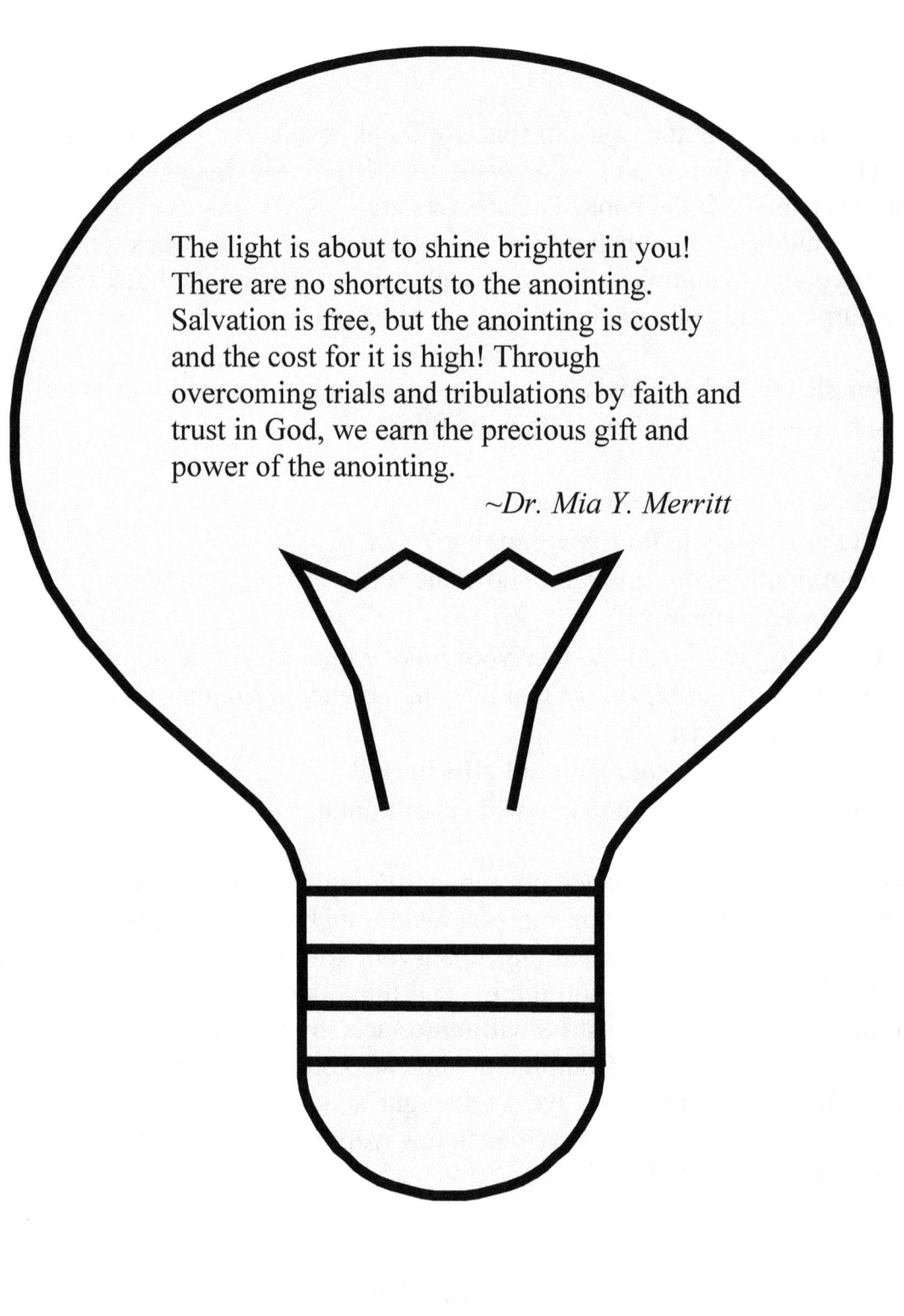

The light is about to shine brighter in you! There are no shortcuts to the anointing. Salvation is free, but the anointing is costly and the cost for it is high! Through overcoming trials and tribulations by faith and trust in God, we earn the precious gift and power of the anointing.

~*Dr. Mia Y. Merritt*

Table of Contents

About This Workbook iii

Chapter 1: In the Will of God 1

Chapter 2: The Fullness of Time 15

Chapter 3: Stepping into Destiny 31

Chapter 4: Spiritual Gifts 43

Chapter 5: The Prosperity Consciousness 57

Chapter 6: Amazing Grace.. 69

Chapter 7: Holding on to His Promises 83

Chapter 8: Victory in Christ 91

About the Author 101

Thou will keep him in perfect peace whose mind is stayed on thee because He trusts in thee (Isaiah 26:3).

Chapter 1

In the Will of God

For our light affliction, which is but for a moment, works for us a far more exceeding and eternal weight of glory; while we look not at the things which are seen, but at the things which are not seen: for the things which are seen are temporal; but the things which are not seen are eternal

(2 Corinthians 4:17-19).

EXCERPTS

◆ Being in God's will does not necessarily mean that you are in His perfect will. Understand that there is the *perfect* will of God and the *permissive* will of God. The permissive will simply means that God is "permitting" you to function in the manner you are operating, even though it is not ultimately His divine plan for your life.

◆ Tests are designed to make us stronger, to examine our fortitude, and to make us wiser. There is always a hidden lesson to be found in every test. God does test us. He has to test the faith that we claim we have in Him.

◆ It is in the wilderness when God reveals Himself to you through your total dependence upon Him. He authenticates you, anoints you, and proves Himself to be your Father. He prepares you and teaches you things that you could not learn in the natural. While in the wilderness, self has to die.

◆ Everyone will endure hardships and disappointments at some point in life, but in the Word of God, these are referred to as "light afflictions." To us, it seems very hard and we wonder how much longer we must suffer, but God who, in His infinite wisdom looks at everything from the perspective of eternity says, "This is a light affliction and you have only endured for a moment."

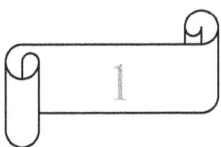

Chapter 1 Activity

Part A: IN HIS WILL

1. In your own words, explain what it means to be in the "Will of God." _____
   _____
   _____
   _____

2. As you reflect on your life right now, do you think you are in God's will? If yes, do you think it is His "permissive" will or His "perfect" will? _____

3. Explain your answer and why you feel that way. _____
   _____
   _____
   _____

4. If you feel that you are in God's PERMISSIVE will and not His PERFECT will, do you desire to be in His perfect will? _____ Are you willing to do what is necessary in order to be in His perfect will? _____

5. If yes, list the things you feel you may need to do in order to get into His PERFECT will. If already in His perfect will, how do you know and how did you get there?

   a) _____
   b) _____
   c) _____
   d) _____
   e) _____

> **Note to Self:** His PERFECT will may mean giving up some habits, some people, some thoughts and some things. Am I really ready for that?

2

Part B: CHOOSING THE RIGHT PATH

> You have your own path to travel and you must travel it. You can take the direct route (straight and narrow) or the scenic route (wide and broad) to get there. Ideally, it should be that the manner in which we evolve will lead to the path where we find ourselves. (pg 3)

1. Considering the above statement, have you been more drawn to the straight and narrow or the broad and wide path throughout your life? _____

2. Why do you think you mostly chose one over the other? _____

3. On a scale of 1-10, ten being highest, how well do you think you have chosen the paths that God has placed before you during your lifetime?

    1 2 3 4 5 6 7 8 9 10

    _____

4. As you reflect back over your life, list two instances where you feel you did NOT choose the right path (this activity is not designed to make you feel bad, but to allow you to see the lessons learned from the experiences).

    First Situation _____

What lesson did you learn from the above situation? _____

Second Situation _____

What lesson did you learn from the second situation? _____

_____

5. Is it easier or more difficult at this stage of your life to choose the straight and narrow path?
_____

   Explain your answer: _____
   _____
   _____

6. Name some of the difficulties that can happen when we choose the wide and broad path (the easy route). _____
_____
_____

7. Name some of the blessings that can happen when we choose the straight and narrow path (the more difficult route). _____
_____
_____

8. Why do you think you are more inclined to choose one more than the other? _____
_____
_____

9. What are some things that you may need to do, get rid of, or pray about in order to help you get on and stay on the right path? _____
_____
_____

Part C: TAILOR-MADE TESTS

> When God desires to take us to the next spiritual level, we must pass our tailor-made test first. When you past the test in the natural, God will bless you in the spirit, but if you fail the test in the natural, you must do your first work all over again. Life is too short to be going around and around the same mountain of trial. (Pg 5)

1. As you reflect back on <u>most</u> of your tailor-made tests/trials/difficulties/ tribulations, grade yourself on how well you think you passed them?   __A __B __C __D __F

2. In being very honest, why did you give yourself the above grade?

_____

_____

_____

3. On the lines below explain one of the worst tests/trials/tribulations/hardships that you ever endured or are enduring.

_____

_____

_____

_____

_____

_____

4. Check how you felt/feel as you were/are going through this situation?

___ sad	___ depressed	___ faithless
___ angry	___ angry with God	___ hopeless
___ bitter	___ frustrated	___ weak
___ disappointed	___ sick	___ helpless
___ rejected	___ alone	___ scared
___ forgotten about	___ confused	___ discouraged

Add your own here. _____ _____ _____

5. As you reflect, was/is this a situation that could have been prevented by you in some way?
   ____ yes   ____ no   ____ not sure   ____ a little of both

6. If no, skip to question 7. If yes, what could you have done to prevent the situation from happening or getting too out of hand? _____
_____
_____
_____

7. Do you feel that God brought/will bring you out of it? _____

8. What lessons did you learn/are you learning from the situation? _____
_____
_____
_____

9. Do you think that you are a better person for having enduring that/this situation? _____.
   If yes, explain how you are (getting) better. If no, explain. _____
_____
_____
_____

10. On a scale of 1-10, how HEALED are you from the experience? _____

11. Please write what you feel it will take to get completely healed from the situation?
_____
_____
_____

Note to self: Tests are not designed to kill me, but to reveal me.

Part D: THE WILDERNESS

> The wilderness is a place of irritation and discomfort. However, it is in the wilderness when God reveals Himself to you through your total dependence upon Him. He authenticates you, anoints you, and proves Himself to be your Father. He prepares you and teaches you things that you could not learn in the natural. (pg. 6)

1. Have you ever had a wilderness experience? ____yes ____no (if no, then keep on living.)

2. If yes, explain what was happening to you as you were in the wilderness.

_____
_____
_____
_____
_____

3. Why do you think you were placed in the wilderness? _____

_____
_____
_____
_____

4. What did God teach you while you were there? _____

_____
_____

5. How were you different when you came out of the wilderness? _____

_____
_____

6. Do you understand why the wilderness is necessary for the believer? Explain your answer.
_____
_____
_____
_____

Part E: THE LIGHT OF KNOWLEDGE

1. Why is it that Satan does not want you to know the will of God for your life? _____
_____
_____

2. What usually happens when you discover God's will for your life and you begin walking in it?
_____
_____

3. What does it mean to become spiritually impregnated? _____
_____
_____

4. What does Satan try to do to the "holy thing" that you are impregnated with? _____
_____
_____

5. What must the believer do in order to stay strong against the enemy when he attacks? _____
_____
_____

6. What happens when you finally give birth to what God has impregnated you with? _____
_____
_____

CHAPTER 1: IN THE WILL OF GOD
On the lines below, journal about the main things that stuck with you from this chapter

Chapter 1 Answer Key

1. In your own words, explain what it means to be in the "Will of God."
   Answers may vary, but may include:
   - ✓ **Being in accordance with God's plan for you**
   - ✓ **Walking on the path that God has presented before you.**
   - ✓ **Being covered under His guidance as He leads you**

2. As you reflect on your life right now, do you think you are in His will? If yes, do you think it is His "permissive" will or His "perfect" will?
   There is no right or wrong answer.

3. Explain your answer and why you feel that way. **Answers will vary**

4. If you feel that you are in God's PERMISSIVE will and not His PERFECT will, do you desire to be in His perfect will? _____ Are you willing to do what is necessary for the perfect will? **Answers may vary**

5. If yes, list the things that you feel you may need to do in order to get into His PERFECT will. **Answers may vary**

Part B: CHOOSING THE RIGHT PATH

1. Considering the above statement, have you been more drawn to the straight and narrow or the broad and wide path throughout your life? **Answers are personal for each person.**
2. Why do you think you mostly chose one over the other? **Answers may vary**
3. On a scale of 1-10, ten being highest, how well do you think you have chosen the paths that God has placed before you during your lifetime? **Answers are personal for each person.**
4. As you reflect back over your life, list two instances where you feel you did not choose the right path (this activity is not designed to make you feel bad, but to get you to see the lessons learned from the experiences). **Answers are personal for each person.**
   What lesson did you learn from that situation? **Answers may vary**
   What lesson did you learn from that situation? **Answers may vary**
5. Is it easier or more difficult at this stage of your life to choose the straight and narrow path? **Answers are personal for each person.**
6. Name some of the difficulties that can happen when we choose the wide and broad path (the easy route). **Answers may vary, but may include:**

   - We end up at a dead end
   - We end up falling into temptation
   - We end up wasting lots of time
   - We can end up in the devil's backyard
   - We end up hurt, discouraged, disappointed and frustrated.

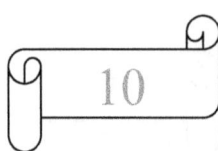

7. Name some of the benefits that can happen when we choose the straight and narrow path (the more difficult route). **Answers may vary, but may include:**

    - ✓ **You avoid many of dangers and pitfall when you choose the straight path**
    - ✓ **You get to your predestined assignment quicker**
    - ✓ **You avoid a lot of disappointments, heartaches and troubles**

8. Why do you think you are more inclined to choose one more than the other? **Answers are personal for each person.**

9. What are some things that you may need to do, get rid of or pray about in order to help you get on and stay on the right path? **Answers may vary, but may include:**

    - ✓ **Releasing some bad habits**
    - ✓ **Changing the company I keep**
    - ✓ **Staying focused on my goals**
    - ✓ **Praying for often**
    - ✓ **Following through on things I start, etc.**

Part C: TAILOR-MADE TESTS

1. As you reflect back on <u>most</u> of your tailor-made tests, grade yourself on how well you think you passed them? __A __B __C __D __F **Answers are personal for each person.**
2. In being very honest, why did you give yourself the above grade? **Answers may vary**
3. On the lines below explain one of the worst tests/trials/tribulations/hardships that you ever endured or are enduring. **Answers are personal for each person.**
4. Check how you felt/feel as you were/are going through this situation? **Answers may vary**

    | ___ sad | ___ depressed | ___ faithless |
    | ___ angry | ___ angry with God | ___ hopeless |
    | ___ bitter | ___ frustrated | ___ weak |
    | ___ disappointed | ___ sick | ___ helpless |
    | ___ rejected | ___ alone | ___ scared |
    | ___ forgotten about | ___ confused | ___ discouraged |

5. As you reflect, was/is this a situation that could have been prevented by you in some way? **Answers may vary**

6. If no, skip to question 7. If yes, what could you have done to prevent the situation from happening or getting too out of hand? **Answers may vary**
7. Do you feel that God brought/will bring you out of it? **Answers will vary**
8. What lessons did you learn/are you learning from the situation? **Answers will vary**
9. Do you think that you are a better person for having endured that/this situation? **Answers will vary**

    If yes, explain how you are (getting) better. If no, explain. **Answers will vary**
10. On a scale of 1-10, how HEALED are you from the experience? **Answers will vary**

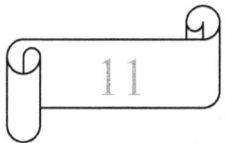

11. Please write what you feel it will take to get completely healed from the situation? **Answers will vary**

Part D: THE WILDERNESS

1. Have you ever had a wilderness experience? ____yes ____no (If no, then keep on living.)
   Answers may vary
2. If yes, how explain what was happening to you as you were in the wilderness.
   Answers may vary
3. Why do you think you were placed there? **Answers may vary**
4. What did God teach you while you were there? **Answers may vary**
5. How were you changed when you came out of the wilderness? **Answers may vary**
6. Do you understand why the wilderness is necessary for the Christian? Explain your answer.
   Answers may vary, but may include:

Part E: THE LIGHT OF KNOWLEDGE

1. Why is it that Satan does not want you to know the will of God for your life? **Answers may vary, but may include:**

   - **Because when you know God's will, you become empowered and you start walking in it**
   - **Satan wants you ignorant and walking in darkness**
   - **As long as you are in darkness concerning God's will for your life, you are not fulfilled**
   - **You become strengthened when you know Gods' will for your life**
   - **Your faith in God increases and Satan does not want you having faith in God.**

2. What usually happens when you discover God's will for your life and you begin walking in it? **Answers may vary, but may include:**
   - **You become empowered, self-assured and confident'**
   - **You begin walking on the straight and narrow path**

3. What does it mean to become spiritually impregnated? **Answers may vary, but may include:**

   - **You become pregnant when you received a revelation from God concerning your life.**
   - **You begin carrying a ministry or great gift that God places inside of you**
   - **You are given a great commission that God is going to use you to carry out.**

4. What does Satan try to do to the "holy thing" that you are impregnated with? **Answers may vary, but may include:**

   - **He wants to cause a spiritual miscarriage, abortion of murder of the "holy thing"**

5. What must the believer do in order to stay strong against the enemy when he attacks? **Answers may vary, but may include:**

    - **Stay in prayer**
    - **Stay in the Word of God**
    - **Fast**

6. What happens when you finally give birth to what God has impregnated you with? **Answers may vary, but may include:**

    - **You are a new creature**
    - **The kingdom of heaven in increased**
    - **You are anointed to do the Work of God**
    - **You are stronger, wiser and strengthened in the Lord.**

Chapter 2
The Fullness of Time

But when the fullness of time was come, God sent forth His Son, made of a woman, made under the law, to redeem them that were under the law, that we might receive the adoption of sons.
(Galatians 4:4-5)

EXCERPTS

◆ We do not need to "help" God in carrying out His will for our lives. He does not need nor want our help. Disastrous things can happen when we grow impatient in waiting on the Lord.

◆ Delayed obedience is disobedience. Do not let the timing pass you by and cause you to miss your divine appointment. Know the seasons and when your time comes, leap out on faith.

◆ Spiritual leaders are called to feed the flock of God, not to set up their own flocks. They are not called to teach about Jesus, but to allow Jesus to teach through them.

◆ You must seek the Lord daily because as you stand before the sheep of God, you must be able to feed them an on-time, in season Word fresh from Heaven. The only way you can do that is by staying in His presence and allowing Him to drop His message into your spirit.

◆ Fashionable sinners are enrolled on the church records, and fashionable sins are concealed under a pretense of Godliness. It suits the policy of Satan that men should retain the "forms" of religion if but the Spirit of vital Godliness is missing.

Chapter 2 Activity

Part A: WAITING

> *But when the fullness of time was come, God sent forth His Son, made of a woman, made under the law, to redeem them that were under the law, that we might receive the adoption of sons.*
> *(Galatians 4:4-5)*

1. Why is it important to WAIT on God? _____
   _____
   _____

2. Have you ever grown impatient in waiting on Him? _____

3. What are some of the things that can happen when we grow impatient in waiting on God and then try to "help" Him? _____
   _____
   _____

4. What should you do when you find yourself growing impatient in waiting on God? _____
   _____
   _____

5. What is the difference between the ANOINTING and the APPOINTING? _____
   _____
   _____
   _____

6. What should the believer be doing in the time between the anointing and the appointing?

_____

_____

_____

7. What is the danger in stepping out before the right time? _____

_____

_____

8. List three reasons why it is important to wait on God and not grow impatient in waiting.

    i. _____

    ii. _____

    iii. _____

9. Write down two scriptures that encourage believers to be patient, wait on the Lord and/or not become anxious.

  i.   Book: _____ chapter _____ Verse: _____ Scripture: _____

_____

_____

  ii.   Book: _____ chapter _____ Verse: _____ Scripture: _____

_____

_____

Part B: SEASONS

> Be not deceived; God is not mocked: for whatsoever a man soweth, that shall he also reap.
> *Galatians 6:7*

1. What is the difference between sowing and reaping? _____
   _____
   _____

2. What kinds of things are you doing when you are sowing? _____
   _____
   _____

3. Have can you tell when its harvest season? _____
   _____
   _____

4. Name at least four things that you should do during SOWING season in order to reap a good harvest for REAPING season.

   i. _____

   ii. _____

   iii. _____

   iv. _____

5. Over the last two years, what kind of seeds do you think you have been sowing? Check all that apply.

   _____ kind seeds   _____ mean seeds   _____ helping seeds   _____ tithing seeds

   _____ sacrificial seeds   _____ praying seeds   _____ honest seeds   _____ dishonest seeds
   (these are in addition to tithing)

   _____ fasting seeds   _____ moody seeds   _____ gossiping seeds   _____ complaining seeds

   _____ nagging seeds   _____ loving seeds   _____ peaceful seeds   _____ sowing discord seeds

   Any additional here: _____ _____ _____

6. As you look over your list, what (if any) seeds do you think you need to add or remove?

_____

_____

7. Are you pleased with the seeds you have been sowing? _____ yes _____ no _____ somewhat

8. Do you think the Lord is happy with the seeds you have been sowing? _____ yes no_____ Explain.

_____

_____

Part C: TEMPTATIONS

> ...and when the devil had ended all the temptations, he departed from him for a season.
>
> (Luke 4:13)

1. Based upon what you have learned in your book, 'The Cost of the Anointing', how many times did the devil tempt Jesus? _____

2. The areas of temptations that we learned about are <u>Identity</u> (basic needs), <u>worship</u>, and the attempt to abort the <u>divine calling</u>. Explain three examples of what is meant by basic needs.

   i. _____

   ii. _____

   iii. _____

3. Why does the devil come and challenge you in the area of your identity when you are lacking in your basic needs? _____

_____

_____

4. Human beings were created to worship. It is imbedded in our very DNA to worship. Name some things that we can end up worshipping if we do not deliberately choose to worship God.

    i. _____

    ii. _____

    iii. _____

    iv. _____

    v. _____

5. Why did Satan use the pleasures of the world to temp Jesus during the 2nd temptation? _____
_____
_____

6. How does the devil tempt the people of God using worldly pleasures as bait? _____
_____
_____

7. The devil comes to steal, kill, destroy, abort, or murder your divine calling. How did he try to temp Jesus in this area? _____
_____
_____

8. In what manner did Jesus respond to Satan in EVERY temptation? _____
_____

9. How should the people of God respond to the devil's temptations? _____
_____

10. Why is it that Satan wants to steal your worship from the Father? _____
_____
_____

11. When you are presented with temptations, what are some things you can do in order to resist?
_____
_____
_____

Note to self: In order to overcome temptations, I must want to resist them. Satan makes the temptations very appealing and if I am not strengthened in the Word of God, I can fall into temptations.

12. As you look back over your life, can you identify the areas where you have been the most tempted in?

    i. _____

    ii. _____

13. As you do self reflections while looking at your list above, why do you think you have struggled in those areas:

    Number i: _____
_____

On a scale of 1-10 how much have you mastered this temptation today? _____

    Number ii: _____
_____

On a scale of 1-10 how much have you mastered this temptation today? _____

14. Is there a particular area of your life that you are still struggling in? If so, what is it? _____
_____
_____

15. Why do you think it is so hard for you to overcome this weakness? _____
_____
_____

16. What do you think you need to do in order to gain victory in this area of temptation? _____
_____
_____

17. Are you willing to make the sacrifice needed in order to overcome this area for 30 consecutive days? _____ If yes, set the date that you are willing to begin, then each day that you resist temptation in this area, put a checkmark (√) in the box for that day.

18. Date I am willing to begin my journey to overcoming my greatest temptation. _____

1. _____	11. _____	21. _____
2. _____	12. _____	22. _____
3. _____	13. _____	23. _____
4. _____	14. _____	24. _____
5. _____	15. _____	25. _____
6. _____	16. _____	26. _____
7. _____	17. _____	27. _____
8. _____	18. _____	28. _____
9. _____	19. _____	29. _____
10. _____	20. _____	30. _____

19. The Bible says that the righteous man falls seven times, but rises up again (Proverbs 24:16). Let's pray that you do NOT fall, but if you do, list the date(s) you fell and write how you are going to be stronger the next time.

Date: _____ Method of resisting. _____

Date: _____ Method of resisting. _____

_____

Date: _____ Method of resisting. _____

_____

> **Note to self:** It has been said that anything done for 30 consecutive days, forms new patterns in the mind that picks up the new thing desired. The less I give in to temptation, the weaker the temptation becomes. Therefore, I will not give in to the devil's temptation, but will read my Bible as I strive to overcome this area of weakness in my life.

Part D: SPIRITUAL LEADERS

1. Who must train you in order for you to receive true spiritual authority? _____

_____

2. Why is it that the great Teacher often passes by the great men of the earth and rests His spirit upon the humble, meek and teachable? _____

_____

_____

3. When you finish the Master's Course, you earn your B.A. Degree. What does this degree stand for?
_____

4. Why is it that churches sometimes choose spiritual leaders that lack the fruit of the spirit or the anointing of God? _____

_____

5. What is the proper way that spiritual leaders should be chosen? _____
_____
_____

6. In heaven, rank is earned by what? _____

7. Why is it that the church awakens no opposition with the world these days? _____
_____
_____

8. What does it mean to have a "form" of Godliness, but to deny the power thereof? ___
_____
_____

9. What happens when the unadulterated, uncompromised and watered down gospel is preached? _____
_____
_____

10. What does it mean by there are no shortcuts to anointed ministry? _____
_____
_____

11. What does it mean to be ANOINTED? _____
_____
_____

CHAPTER 2: THE FULLNESS OF TIME

On the lines below, journal about the main things that stuck with you from this chapter

Chapter 2 Answer Key

Part A: WAITING

1. What is it important to WAIT on God? **Answers may vary, but may include:**

   - Because God knows the perfect time for your life
   - Because all things work together for good for those who love God
   - Because God has called us to be patient and be anxious for nothing

2. Have you ever grown impatient in waiting on Him? **No right or wrong answer Answers may vary, but may include:**

   - We can end up trying to "help" Him and make major mistakes
   - We can cause a life of misery trying to find the answer on our own
   - We can become frustrated and begin doubting Him

3. What is the difference between the ANOINTING and the APPOINTING?

   The **anointing** is when you get the revelation of what God has called you to do from God Himself or the messenger of God.

   The **appointing** is the time when you actually begin walking in the destiny that God has spoken over you.

4. What should the believer be doing in the time between the anointing and the appointing? **Answers may vary, but may include:**

   - **Studying the position**
   - **Praying**
   - **Studying the scriptures**
   - **Seeking the Lord**
   - **Fasting**

5. What is the danger in stepping out before the right time? **Answers may vary, but may include:**

   - We can become cheap imitations of others
   - We can end up in humiliation
   - We are not ready to be presented and can fall a hard fall

6. List three reasons why it is important to wait on God and not grow impatient in waiting. **Answers may vary, but may include:**

   It is important to wait on God because our patience is enhanced when we do
   It is important to wait on God because His timing is always perfect
   It is important to wait on God because our Faith in Him increases

7. Write down two scriptures that encourage believers to be patient, wait on the Lord and/or not become anxious (be sure to include the book, chapter and verse). **Answers will vary.**

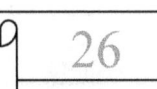

Part B: SEASONS

1. What is the difference between sowing and reaping? **Answers may vary, but may include:**

    Sowing is when you are planting seeds. Reaping is when you are getting a return on the seeds that you have planted.

2. What kinds of things are you doing when you are sowing? **Answers may vary, but may include:**

    Examples of sowing can be paying tithes, volunteering, preparing sermons, visiting the sick, feeding the homeless, serving in ministry, etc.

3. Have can you tell when its harvest season? **Answers may vary, but may include:**

    Harvest is when blessings come from nowhere, promotions are given, favor is manifested into your life.

4. Name at least four things that you need to do during SOWING season in order to reap a good harvest for REAPING season. **Answers may vary, but may include:**

    Examples of sowing can be paying tithes, volunteering, preparing sermons, visiting the sick, feeding the homeless, serving in ministry, etc.

5. Over the last two years, what kind of seeds do you think you have been sowing? Check all that apply. **Answers will vary.**
6. As you look over your list, what (if any) things do you think you need to change? **Answers will vary.**
7. Are you pleased with the seeds that you have been sowing? **Answers will vary.**
8. Do you think the Lord is happy with the seeds you have been sowing? **Answers will vary.**

Part C: TEMPTATIONS

1. Based upon what we have learned in the above scripture and in your book, 'The Cost of the Anointing', how many times did the devil tempt Jesus? **Three times**

2. The areas of temptations that we learned about are Identity (basic needs), worship, and the divine calling. Explain three examples of what is meant by basic needs.

    Basic needs are those things we cannot live without such as food, shelter, water, clothing, money, companionship, etc.

3. Why does the devil come and challenge you in the area of your identity when you are lacking in your basic needs? **Answers may vary, but may include:**

- **Because he wants you to begin doubting God. "If you were a child of God, then why is he allowing this to happen to you?**
- **Because he knows that you are in need right at that moment and are more inclined to compromise**
- **Because he wants you to turn from God.**

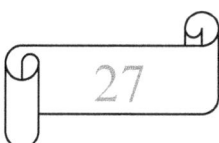

4. Human beings were created to worship. It is imbedded in our very DNA to worship. Name some things that we can end up worshipping if we do not choose to worship God. **Answers may vary, but may include:**

Your house, your car, money, position, spouse, children, name, etc.

5. Why did the devil use the pleasures of the world to temp Jesus during the 2nd temptation? **Answers may vary, but may include:**

- **Because he knows that many humans are worldly minded and are attracted to the pleasures of this world.**
- **Jesus was raised in poverty and may be appealed by having nice things, etc.**

6. How does the devil tempt the people of God using worldly pleasures as bait? **Answers may vary, but may include:**

- **Because he knows that when we are in lack in a particular area, we may be attracted to the appearance of being delivered from the situation.**
- **Because he knows that those who are worldly-minded are attracted to worldly things and respect those who have them**
- **Because he knows that worldly things gives an appearance of prosperity, thus drawing the respect and homage of men.**

7. The devil comes to steal, abort, or murder your divine calling. How did he try to temp Jesus in this area?

- **He wanted Jesus to jump off of the high mountain, which was not part of the plan of redemption for mankind. This would have intercepted the plan to redeem the lost world back to God.**

8. In what manner did Jesus respond to Satan in every temptation? **With the words, "It is written".**
9. How should the people of God respond to the devil's temptations? **With the words, "It is written".**
10. Why is it that Satan wants to steal your worship from the Father? **Because he has been in the throne room and he desires worship for himself.**

11. When you are presented with temptations, what are some things that you can do in order to resist? **Answers may vary, but may include:**

- **Use the words, "It is written" then quote relevant scriptures that will help you hold on to the Word of God.**
- **Try and remove yourself from the tempting situation if possible.**
- **Pray and ask the Holy Spirit to strengthen you in the area of your weakness.**

12. As I look back over my life, I see that I have been tempted in the following areas the most. **Answers will vary.**
13. As I do some self reflection while looking at the list above, below is why I think I have struggled in those areas: **Answers will vary.**

On a scale of 1-10 how much have you mastered this temptation today? **Answers will vary.**

14. Is there a particular area of your life that you are still struggling in? if so, what is it? **Answers will vary.**

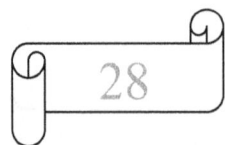

15. Why do you think it is so hard for you to overcome this weakness? **Answers will vary.**
16. What do you think you need to do in order to gain the victory over this area of temptation? **Answers will vary.**
17. Are you willing to make the sacrifice needed in order to overcome this area for 30 consecutive days? _____ If yes, set the date that you are going to begin, then each day that you resist temptation in this area, put a checkmark (√) in the box for that day. **Answers and start dates will vary.**
18. Date I am willing to begin my journey to overcoming my greatest temptation. **No right or wrong answers**
19. The Bible says, that the righteous man falls seven times, but rises up again. Let's pray you do NOT fall, but if you do, list the date(s) and write how you are going to be stronger the next time. **Answers will vary.**

Part C: SPIRITUAL LEADERS

1. Who must train you in order for you to receive true spiritual authority? **God must train you Himself**
2. Why is it that the great Teacher often passes by the great men of the earth and rests His spirit upon the humble, meek and teachable? **Answers may vary, but may include the fact that:**

- **The humble, meek and teachable are open to receiving from the Lord**
- **They are not accustomed to receiving praise and respect from men**
- **They don't think they know it all**
- **They are not caught up in pride**

3. When you finish the Master's Course, you earn your B.A. Degree. What does this degree stand for?

   Born Again!

4. Why is it that churches sometimes choose spiritual leaders that lack the fruit of the spirit or the anointing of God? Answers may vary, but may include:

- **Because they are impressed by what theses leaders have accomplished in the world instead of being lead of the spirit**
- **Because these leaders have the ability to draw a large crowd**
- **Because these leaders are charismatic and articulate**
- **Because these leaders have connections.**

5. What is the proper way that spiritual leaders should be chosen? **They should be led by the spirit of God. Those choosing to be sensitive to the Spirit as to whom He has chosen and pray about it.**
6. In heaven, rank is earned by what? **Humility and service**
7. Why is it that the church awakens no opposition with the world these days? **Because they have resorted to compromise; they do what the world does and there is no distinguishing between the world and the believers.**
8. What does it mean to have a "form" of Godliness, but to deny the power thereof?

This means that on the outside, some want to "appear" that they are believers. They go to church, pray with, sing with, and act like true believers, but their hearts are far from God.

9. What happens when the unadulterated, uncompromised and watered down gospel is preached?
People are set free from the grips of sin and flames of hell; they are then able to take the narrow path that leads to the unfoldment of the destiny.

10. What does it mean by there are no shortcuts to anointed ministry?
There is only one way to the anointing and that is through tests, trials, tribulations, hardships, difficulties, the wilderness and/or the fire. That is the only way one can be purged so that the Spirit of the Lord can rest upon them.

11. What does it mean to be ANOINTED? Being anointed can have two meanings, which are:
- **Being called and chosen by God to do a work for the kingdom**
- **Having the spirit and power of God resting upon you.**

Chapter 3
Stepping into Destiny

> *...moreover whom he did predestinate, them He also called: and whom he called, them he also justified: and whom he justified, them he also glorified.*
>
> (Romans 8:30)

EXCERPTS

♦ You do not have to confess your weakness in your humanity, but rather declare your strength, which is in divinity.

♦ There is a present truth for this time, but you can only discover what it is by diligently, earnestly and consistently studying the scriptures.

♦ Christ was treated as we deserve so that we could be treated as He deserves. He was condemned for our sins, in which He had no share, so that we could be justified by His righteousness, in which we had no share.

♦ Faith is like a toothbrush, everybody should have one and use it daily, but they should not try to use someone else's. Faith is not like gasoline which runs out as you use it, but like a muscle, which grows stronger as you exercise it.

♦ There are three different kinds of wisdom: human wisdom, worldly wisdom, and Godly wisdom.

Chapter 3 Activity

Part A: REMEMBER

> As you look back over your life, can't you see that God never left you even though there were times when you thought He had? He proved Himself to be right there all along. (p.33)

1. Why is it important to look back over your life and remember how far God has brought you?

_____

_____

2. Why is it important to share your testimony with others? _____

_____

_____

3. When you look back over your life and remember your trials and struggles, do you believe that it was God who delivered you out of them? Explain your answer_____

_____

_____

_____

Part B: REJOICE

> We rejoice because that same "I AM" God is the same yesterday, today and forever. He changes not. We have access to Him and for this reason, we rejoice! (pg 34)

1. When God said to Moses, *Thus shall you say unto the children of Israel, I AM has sent me to you (Exodus 3:13)*. What did God mean by his name is "I AM"? _____

_____

_____

2. When you speak the words, "**I AM**…" you are identifying yourself with God, therefore everything that comes behind "I am", should be good, prosperous, loving and blessed words. What are some words that you can speak about yourself that you want to see manifested when you say "I am"?

I am _____ I am _____ I am _____

I am _____ I am _____ I am _____

I am _____ I am _____ I am _____

> **Note to Self:** We must never forget what God has done for us because it gives us the assurance in knowing that He will always be there.

3. On the lines below, list as many reasons as you can to rejoice.

i. _____

ii. _____

iii _____

iv. _____

v. _____

**WE HAVE MORE REASONS TO REJOICE
THAN WE HAVE TO COMPLAIN!**

The first time that God identified himself was in Exodus 3:13. However, we have learned that there are other names for God written in Hebrew language. Try and match the Hebrews names for God on the right to their proper translation on the left.

Adonai	_____	A	The Lord our righteousness
El Elyon	_____	B	The plural form of God
El Olam	_____	C	The Lord My Shepherd
El Shaddai	_____	D	Lord, Master
Elohim	_____	E	The Everlasting God
Jehovah Jireh	_____	F	The Lord of Hosts
Jehovah Nissi	_____	G	The Lord who provides
Jehovah Raah	_____	H	The Most High God
Jehovah Rapha	_____	I	The Lord that heals
Jehovah Sabaoth	_____	J	The Lord God Almighty
Jehovah Shalom	_____	K	The Lord my banner
Jehovah Shammah	_____	L	The Lord is there
Jehovah Tsidkenu	_____	M	The Lord our peace

Part C: REDEDICATE

1. Was there a time in your life that you were much closer to the Lord than you are now? _____

2. If yes, what do you think happened to the motivation and the zeal that you had for Jesus? If no, explain your answer. _____

_____

3. What are some things that you can do to **REDEDICATE** yourself to the Lord?

   i. _____

   ii. _____

   iii. _____

   iv. _____

   v. _____

4. What date are you going to start applying the things listed above? _____

Part D: RENEW

1. As you review the course of your life, are there some areas that have gotten stale, dull, boring, or mundane? If so list those things below (worship, relationship, job-related, etc.).

   i. _____

   ii. _____

   iii. _____

   iv. _____

2. What things can you begin doing right away to renew those areas listed above?

   i. _____

   ii. _____

   iii. _____

   iv. _____

3. What date are you going to begin the renewal process for the things listed above? _____

4. On a scale of 1-10, ten being highest, how much faith do you have in God for even the most difficult challenges?

   1 2 3 4 5 6 7 8 9 10

5. If you circled **five or below**, please express why your faith in God is low. Honesty is growth.

_____

_____

_____

6. If you circled between **6-8**, explain why you feel your faith in God is somewhat high, but not at the highest.

_____

_____

_____

7. If you circled **8-10**, explain how your faith level got to be so high and what you feel believers should do to get to that level of faith. _____

_____

_____

8. Why is it that our promises are sometimes delayed? _____

_____

_____

9. Why is it that some churches do not preach on sin and the destruction of sin as much as they should?

_____

_____

_____

10. How does NOT preaching and teaching about the destructions of sin hurt the body of Christ? _____

_____

_____

11. What can happen to the body of Christ when preachers lovingly begin preaching about sin and holiness?

_____

_____

_____

12. How has your faith in God helped you in your Christian walk? _____

_____

_____

13. Please list below, two things that you are believing God for by faith.

    I. _____

What will you do while you are waiting?_____
_____

        II. _____

What will you do while you are waiting?_____
_____

Faith is the substance of things hoped for, the evidence of things NOT seen!

~Hebrews 11:1

CHAPTER 3: STEPPING INTO DESTINY

On the lines below, journal about the main things that stuck with you from this chapter

Chapter 3 Answer Key

1. Why is it important to look back over your life and remember how far God has brought you? **Answers may vary, but may include:**

   - **So you can have faith that God will always bring you out.**
   - **So you can look back over your life and see how far you have come.**
   - **So that you can testify of His goodness to someone else.**
   - **So that you can be a witness that God never forsakes his children.**

2. Why is it important to share your testimony with others? **Answers may vary, but may include:**

   - **So that you can encourage them through your story.**
   - **So that they can see that there are others who were in their same shoes, but God delivered them and can do the same for themselves.**

3. When you look back over your life and remember your trials and struggles do you believe that it was God who delivered you out of them? Explain your answer. **There are no right or wrong answers.**

Part B: REJOICE

> We rejoice because that same "I AM" God is the same yesterday, today and forever. He changes not. We have access to Him and for this reason, we rejoice! (pg 34)

1. When God said to Moses, *Thus shall you say unto the children of Israel, I AM has sent me to you (Exodus 3:13).* What did God mean by his name is "I AM"?

   - **He meant that He is EVERYTHING that they needed Him to be.**

2. When you speak the words, "I am…" you are identifying yourself with God, therefore everything that comes behind "I am", should be good, prosperous, loving and blessed words. What are some words that you can speak about yourself that you want to see manifested when you say "I am"? **Answers may vary but may include:**

   I "AM" healthy; I "AM" prosperous; I "AM" successful; I "AM" blessed; I "AM" faithful;

3. On the lines below, list as many reasons as you can to rejoice. **Answers will vary.**

The first time that God identified himself was in Exodus 3:13. However, we have learned that there are other names for God written in Hebrew language. Try and match the Hebrews names for God on the right to their proper definition on the left.

Adonai	D	A	The Lord our righteousness
El Elyon	H	B	The plural form of God
El Olam	E	C	The Lord My Shepherd
El Shaddai	J	D	Lord, Master
Elohim	B	E	The Everlasting God
Jehovah Jireh	G	F	The Lord of Hosts
Jehovah Nissi	K	G	The Lord who provides
Jehovah Raah	C	H	The Most High God
Jehovah Rapha	I	I	The Lord that heals
Jehovah Sabaoth	F	J	The Lord God Almighty
Jehovah Shalom	M	K	The Lord my banner
Jehovah Shammah	L	L	The Lord is there
Jehovah Tsidkenu	A	M	The Lord our peace

Part C: REDEDICATE

1. Was there a time in your life that you were much closer to the Lord than you are now? **Answers will vary.**

2. If yes, what do you think happened to the motivation and the zeal that you had for Jesus? **Answers will vary.**

3. What are some things that you can do to REDEDICATE yourself to him? **Answers will vary, but may include:**

- **Start back praying consistently**
- **Read the Bible Consistently**
- **Repent of any unconfessed sins**
- **Begin fasting, etc.**

4. What date are you going to start applying the things listed above? **Answer will vary.**

Part D: RENEW

1. As you review the course of your life, are there some areas that have gotten stale, dull, boring, or mundane? If so list those things below. (worship, relationship, job-related, etc.) **Answers will vary.**

- **Start back praying consistently**
- **Read the Bible Consistently**
- **Repent of any unconfessed sins**
- **Begin fasting, etc.**

2. What things can you begin doing right away to renew those areas listed above? **Answers will vary, but may include.**

- **Start back praying consistently**
- **Read the Bible Consistently**
- **Repent of any unconfessed sins**
- **Begin fasting, etc.**

3. What date are you going to begin the renewal process for the things listed above? **Answer will vary.**

4. On a scale of 1-10 (ten being highest) how much faith do you have in God for even the most difficult challenges? **Answer will vary.**

1 2 3 4 5 6 7 8 9 10

5. If you circled five or below, please express why your faith in God is so low. Honesty is growth. **Answer will vary.**

6. If you circled between 6-8, explain why you feel your faith is somewhat high, but not at the highest. **Answer will vary.**

7. If you circled 8-10, explain how your faith level got to be so high and what you feel believers should do to get to that level of faith. **Answer will vary.**

8. Why is it that our promises are sometimes delayed? **Answer will vary, but may include:**

- **Because evil forces intercept the blessings when they are on the way**
- **Angels have to fight demons when they are in route to delivering the blessings**
- **Principalities and powers try to stop the prayers from going up to the throne room**
- **Because we don't enter spiritual warfare to release our answered prayers, etc.**

9. Why is it that some churches do not preach on sin and the destruction of sin as much and as frequent as they should? **Answer will vary, but may include:**

- **Because they don't want to offend anyone**
- **Because they don't want to lose members**
- **Because they may be sinning themselves**
- **Because they want to preach popular sermons, etc.**

10. How does NOT preaching and teaching about the destructions of sin hurt the body of Christ? **Answer will vary, but may include:**

- **It enables believers to continue in sin not realizing that they are getting deeper in bondage.**
- **Believers are not getting a word that will set them free**
- **Believers are not being taught about the grace in Christ through turning from sin**

11. What can happen to the body of Christ when preachers lovingly begin preaching about sin and holiness? **Answer will vary, but may include:**

- **People become enlightened and give their lives fully to Christ**
- **Individuals begin embracing holiness**

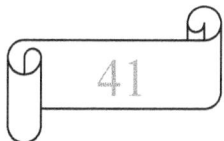

- **People turn from sin and to the power of the Cross**
- **People begin studying the scriptures more and begin walking the straight and narrow.**

12. How has your faith in God helped you in your Christian walk? **Answers will vary.**

13. Below, list some two things that you are believing God for by faith. **Answers will vary.**
    This is what I can do by faith while I am waiting: **Answers will vary.**
    This is what I can do by faith while I am waiting: **Answers will vary.**

Chapter 4

Spiritual Gifts

> *Having then gifts differing according to the grace that is given to us, whether prophecy, let us prophesy according to the proportion of faith; or ministry, let us wait on our ministering: or he that teaches, on teaching; or he that exhorts, on exhortation: he that gives, let him do it with simplicity; he that rules, with diligence; he that shows mercy, with cheerfulness*
>
> *(Romans 12:6-8).*

EXCERPTS

◆ There are three *types* of gifts: motivation, ministry and manifestation and seven motivation gifts. Every believer has only one motivation gift, which is the driving force of everything you do.

◆ Just as we have five physical senses that allow us to function effectively in the natural realm, we also have nine gifts of the Holy Spirit that allow us to function effectively in the spiritual realm.

◆ There are three types of wisdom: the wisdom of God (1 Corinthians 2:6-7); the wisdom of man (Ecclesiastes 1:16-18); and the wisdom of the world (1 Corinthians 2:6).

◆ If you want the gift of miracles to operate in you, then be sure that you have the Word of God in you. Miracles are the product of the spoken Word of God because the Word of God and God are one.

Chapter 4 Activity

Part A: MOTIVATION GIFTS

> There are spiritual gifts that we are not born with, but obtain after we are "born again." Just as you are born of the flesh with a natural gift inside you, when you are "born again" you receive a spiritual motivational gift inside and there are no gifts as precious as God's spiritual gifts. (pg 45)

1. When you are born, you have two things on the inside of you. What are those two things?

   i. _____

   ii. _____

2. Based upon what you have learned, what is the difference between a natural gift and a spiritual gift?
_____
_____

3. Do you know what your natural gift is? ___yes ___no. If yes, explain what it is and how you know this is your gift (or one of them). _____
_____
_____

4. You have learned that your motivational gift is what dominates your behavior and helps you to understand yourself better. Looking at the list below, which one do you believe is your motivational gift? If you feel you have a secondary motivational gift, circle that one as well. Do not circle more than two gifts.

   1. Exhorting
   2. Giving
   3. Ministry
   4. Prophecy
   5. Ruling
   6. Showing Mercy
   7. Teaching

5. Explain why you think this (or these two) is/are your dominating motivational gift.

_____

_____

_____

Part B: FRUIT OF THE SPIRIT

> Many Christians seek the Gifts of the Spirit without first acquiring and exemplifying the Fruit of the Spirit in their lives. We must have the Fruit of the Spirit at work in our lives first, if we want God to entrust us with the Gifts of the Spirit. (pg 47)

1. In looking at the nine fruits of the spirit, put in order from greatest to least the ones that you display the most in your daily life.

THE FRUIT OF THE SPIRIT	THE FRUIT OF THE SPIRIT DISPLAYED IN MY LIFE THE MOST:
Love	
Joy	
Peace	
Longsuffering	
Faith	
Goodness	
Gentleness	
Meekness	
Temperance (self-control)	

2. Which two fruits do you find the easiest to demonstrate in your life?

_____

_____

3. What two fruits do you find the hardest to display in your life?

_____

_____

4. In looking at the last <u>four</u> fruits from your list in the box, which ones are lacking the most in your Christian walk? _____

_____

5. In what situations do you find that you need to display the last four fruits on your list the most?

_____

_____

6. What are you willing to do in order to demonstrate these four fruit more often in your life?

_____

_____

Part C: SPIRITUAL GIFTS

> Just as we have five physical senses that allow us to function effectively in the natural realm, we also have nine gifts of the Holy Spirit that allow us to function effectively in the spiritual realm. The main purpose of spiritual gifts is to manifest the supernatural goals of God.

1. From what you can remember, what are the nine spiritual gifts? List them below (from memory).

1._____   4._____   7._____
2._____   5._____   8._____
3._____   6._____   9._____

2. According to what you have learned, what is the purpose of Spiritual Gifts?

_____

_____

3. Which three gifts are considered "**Revelation**" Gifts? (they reveal)

      i. _____

      ii. _____

      iii. _____

4. Which three gifts are considered "**Power**" Gifts (they show action)?

      i. _____

      ii. _____

      iii. _____

5. Which three gifts are considered "**Inspiration**" Gifts (they say something)?

      i. _____

      ii. _____

      iii. _____

6. We have learned that there are three different kinds of faith. What are they?

      i. _____

      ii. _____

      iii. _____

7. Of the three different kinds of faith, which one gets you into heaven? _____

8. Of the three different kinds of faith, which one gets heaven into you? _____

9. Of the three different kinds of faith, which one gives you the unwavering ability to believe in the miraculous? _____

10. In your book, you learned about the different areas of healing. What are the three different areas of healing?

        i. _____
       ii. _____
      iii. _____

11. Of the nine spiritual gifts, which one (or two) would you like to have?

        i. _____

Which fruit of the spirit is connected to this gift? _____

       ii. _____

Which fruit of the spirit is connected to this gift? _____

12. Why would you like to have this/these gifts? _____

_____

_____

> These gifts can be yours for the asking. No particular gifts are exclusive to any group of people, but they are available to the believer who earnestly desires to have them. P. 57

13. What do you need to do in order to receive the spiritual gift(s) that you desire?

_____

_____

14. On the line below, write the date that you receive the spiritual gift that you are praying for (or the day or month that you realize you have it.) _____

Part D: THE GIFT OF TONGUES

> *And they were all filled with the Holy Ghost, and began to speak with other tongues, as the Spirit gave them utterance. (Acts 2:4)*

1. According to the scripture above, the gift of tongues is the evidence of what? _____
   _____
   _____

2. If a person does not speak in tongues, does that mean they do not have the Holy Spirit? _____

3. Match the definition with the type of tongue listed below:

   A.) An unknown tongue (1 Corinthians 14:2).

   ____ This is a sign to unbelievers (1 Corinthians 14:2; Acts 2:6). This may be unknown to the one speaking, but known to people in a far away country.

   B.) A known tongue

   ____ This tongue is understood through interpretation and edifies the church.

   C.) A interpreted tongue

   ____ This type of tongue edifies you, assists you in prayer during personal prayer time, stirs up the prophetic ministry in you, refreshes your soul, gives victory over the devil, brings you into the presence of God, aids you in intercession, and helps you worship in the Spirit.

4. Based upon what you have learned, speaking in tongues serves two functions. What are the two functions?

   i. _____

   ii. _____

5. If you desire to receive the gift of speaking in tongues, what are the steps that you should take?

   i. _____

   ii. _____

   iii. _____

   iv. _____

   v. _____

6. Below is a prayer that you can pray to God for the spiritual gift that you desire. On the lines below, tell the Lord the gift you would like to have and ask Him for it in writing. Write as though the Lord is going to read this request. Ask in faith, humility and in assurance that He is going to bless you with this gift.

_____

_____

_____

_____

_____

_____

_____

_____

_____

_____

_____

_____

Chapter 4: "SPIRITUAL GIFTS"

On the lines below, journal about the main things that stuck with you from this chapter

Chapter 4 Answer Key

Part A: MOTIVATION GIFTS

> There are spiritual gifts that we are not born with, but obtain after we are "born again." Just as you are born of the flesh with a natural gift inside you, when you are "born again" you receive a spiritual motivational gift inside and there are no gifts as precious as God's spiritual gifts. (pg 45)

1. When you are born, you have two things on the inside of you. What are those two things?

   - **A gift**
   - **An assignment**

2. Based upon what you have read in the book, what is the difference between a natural gift and a spiritual gift?

   - **A natural gift is what every person comes into the world with on the inside of them.**
   - **A spiritual gift is given to us AFTER we are born again.**

3. Do you know what your natural gift is? ___yes ___no. If yes, explain what it is and how you know this is your gift (or one of them). **Answers will vary.**

4. You have learned that your motivational gift helps you to understand other people and yourself better. Looking at the list below, which one do you believe is your motivational gift? Circle it. **Answers will vary.**

   1. Exhorting
   2. Giving
   3. Ministry
   4. Prophecy
   5. Ruling
   6. Showing Mercy
   7. Teaching

5. Explain why you think this is your dominating motivational gift. **Answers will vary.**

Part B: FRUIT OF THE SPIRIT

> Many Christians seek the Gifts of the Spirit without first acquiring and exemplifying the Fruit of the Spirit in their lives. We must have the Fruit of the Spirit at work in our lives first, if we want God to entrust us with the Gifts of the Spirit. (pg 47)

1. In looking at the nine fruits of the spirit. Put in order from greatest to least the ones that you display the most. **Answers will vary.**

THE FRUIT OF THE SPIRIT	THE ORDER OF THE FRUIT OF THE SPIRIT DISPLAYED IN MY LIFE:
Love	
Joy	
Peace	
Longsuffering	
Faith	
Goodness	
Gentleness	
Meekness	
Temperance (self-control)	

2. Which two fruits do you find the easiest to display? **Answers will vary.**
3. What two fruits do you find the hardest for you to display? **Answers will vary.**
4. In looking at the last <u>four</u> fruits from your list in the box, which ones seem to need the most help? **Answers will vary.**
5. In what situations do you find that you need to display the last four fruits on your list the most? **Answers will vary.**
6. What are you willing to do in order to demonstrate these four fruit more often in your life? **Answers will vary.**

Part C: SPIRITUAL GIFTS

1. From what you can remember, what are the nine spiritual gifts? List them below (from memory at first). **Answers will vary.**

Revelation Gifts (gifts that reveal)
    Word of Wisdom
    Word of Knowledge
    Discerning of Spirits

Power Gifts (gifts that show action)
    Faith
    Healing
    Miracles

Inspiration Gifts (gifts that say something)
    Prophecy
    Divers Tongues
    Interpretation of Tongues

2. What is the purpose of Spiritual Gifts? **Answers will vary, but may include the following:**

- **Spiritual gifts help you to become stronger in your prayer life**
- **They help to edify others and yourself**
- **They strengthen you in prayer**
- **They assist you in spiritual warfare**
- **They are the evidence to the world that you are a believer**

3. Which three gifts are considered "Revelation" Gifts?

   1. **Word of Wisdom**
   2. **Word of Knowledge**
   3. **Discerning of Spirits**

4. Which three gifts are considered "Power" Gifts (they show action)?

   1. **Faith**
   2. **Healings**
   3. **Miracles**

5. Which three gifts are considered "Inspiration" Gifts (they say something)?

   1. **Prophecy**
   2. **Divers Tongues**
   3. **Interpretation of Tongues**

6. We have learned that there are three different kinds of faith. What are they?

   1. **Saving faith**

2. Fruit of faith
   3. Gift of faith

7. Of the three different kinds of faith, which one gets you into heaven? **Saving faith**
8. Of the three different kinds of faith, which one gets heaven into you? **Fruit of faith**
9. Of the three different kinds of faith, which one gives you the unwavering ability to believe in the miraculous? **Gift of Faith (one of the spiritual gifts)**

10. In your book, you learned about different areas of healing. What are the three different areas of healing?
    1. **Physical healings**
    2. **Emotional healings**
    3. **Spiritual healings**

11. Of the nine spiritual gifts, which one (or two) would you like to have? **Answers will vary.**

    Which fruit of the spirit is connected to this gift? **Answers will vary.**
    Which fruit of the spirit is connected to this gift? **Answers will vary.**

12. Why would you like to have this/these gifts? **Answers will vary.**
13. What do you need to do in order to receive the spiritual gift(s) that you desire?

    - **Pray and ask God for them.**
    - **Ask God to show you anything that may hinder you from receiving them**
    - **Confess all sins you may have committed.**
    - **Wait on the Holy Spirit to impart you with the gift you have asked for**

14. On the line below, write the date that you receive the spiritual gift that you are desiring (or the day that you realize you have it.) **Answers will vary.**

Part D: THE GIFT OF TONGUES

1. According to the scripture above, the gift of tongues is the evidence of what?

    The gift of tongues is the EVIDENCE of the Holy Spirit in believer's life.

2. If a person does not speak in tongues, does that mean they do not have the Holy Spirit? **No.**

3. Match the definition with the type of tongue listed below:

    A.) An unknown tongue (1 Corinthians 14:2).

    B.) A known tongue

    B This is a sign to unbelievers (1 Corinthians 14:2; Acts 2:6). This may be unknown to the one speaking, but known to people in a far away country.

    C. This tongue is understood through interpretation and edifies the church.

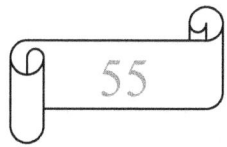

  C.) A interpreted tongue

    A. This type of tongue edifies you, assists you in prayer during personal prayer time, stirs up the prophetic ministry in you, refreshes your soul, gives victory over the devil, brings you into the presence of God, aids you in intercession, and helps you worship in the Spirit.

4. Based upon what you have learned, speaking in tongues serves two functions. What are the two functions?

  1. **Personal** - for your personal prayer life to build you up and help usher you into the gift of prophecy. (No interpretation is necessary when used in this manner.)

  2. **Public** - a direct message in tongues followed by an interpretation. This is for the edification of the church and requires an interpreter.

5. If you desire to receive the gift of speaking in tongues, then follow these steps below:

  vi. Read Acts 2:1-15 and 1 Corinthians 14:5-15
  vii. Ask the Lord to show you any unforgiveness or any other hindrance you may have that can prevent you from receiving the gift.
  viii. Repent and ask God to heal you in those areas and help you to overcome them
  ix. Ask for forgiveness for any sins that may have been committed, then repent of those sins.
  x. Pray for the gift of speaking in tongues as often as you feel it necessary to ask.
  xi. Thank God in advance for blessing you with this valuable gift.

6. Below is a prayer that you can pray for the gift of speaking in tongues.

Heavenly Father, in Jesus' name, I humbly ask You to stir up the gift of tongues in me by the Power of your Holy Ghost. Remove all obstacles in the way of me receiving my gift. Allow me to use my tongues to communicate with you out of my spirit, refresh my soul, strengthen me, and to worship you in Spirit and in Truth. I thank you by faith for what you have already done. In the name of Jesus, I pray. Amen.

Now, thank and praise the Lord for what is already done in the Spirit. Allow the manifestation to come forth. Open your mouth and speak. Then obediently extend your expressions of love by praying and thanking Him in tongues.

Chapter 5

The Prosperity Consciousness

Beloved, I wish above all things that thou may prosper and be in health, even as thy soul prospers.
(3 John 1:2-3)

EXCERPTS

- There Prosperity is a mindset and begins in the mind. Once the mind has been saturated in the understanding of the laws of prosperity, the embodiment of that revelation is manifested in the outward life.

- God is not going to entrust you with thousands of dollars if you have not been faithful with hundreds and He definitely will not entrust you with millions if you have not been faithful with thousands.

- The wealthy have certain patterns of thinking that draws money to them. Their minds are a magnet for money because they have the money consciousness. If people in your town, your city, your state, and your country can become rich, then so can you.

- At different seasons, the tide of opportunity sets in different directions according to the needs of the whole. When the tides advance, there is prosperity; when they recede, there is a recession.

Chapter 5 Activity

PART A: PROSPERITY

> Prosperity is connected to spiritual laws and principles and it is essential to understand what those laws and principles are so that people will not be ignorant as to why they are constantly struggling. Pg. 63

1. Based on what you have read, what is your definition of prosperity? _____
_____
_____

2. Is it possible for someone to have inherited a million dollars and still not be prosperous? Explain.
_____
_____

3. Write a scripture from the bible that has to do with prosperity. Be sure to include the chapter and verse.
_____
_____

4. In your opinion, is it a sin to be rich? ___yes ___no; Explain. _____
_____
_____

5. In your opinion, is it a sin to be poor? ___yes ___no; Explain. _____
_____

6. Is it possible to be cursed and rich? ___yes ___no; Explain. _____

_____

_____

7. Is it possible to be poor and blessed? ___yes ___no; Explain. _____

Part B: PROSPERITY LINKS

> There is an anointing for prosperity and once you are able to tap into that anointing, you will never be in poverty or lack another day of your life. Just as you grow and are elevated in the knowledge and wisdom of Christ Jesus and are able to enter into the throne room through prayers, supplication and a humble heart, you can also enter into the spiritual realm where prosperity permeates. (pg 67)

1. Prosperity is linked to my _____. Explain. _____

_____

_____

2. Prosperity is linked to my _____. Explain. _____

_____

_____

3. Prosperity is linked to my _____. Explain. _____

_____

_____

4. Prosperity is linked to my _____. Explain. _____

_____

Part C: RECOGNITION

> Your prosperity anointing is linked to your ability to recognize certain things. Recognition can mean the same thing as discernment. Ask the Lord for clear vision to be able to recognize opportunities, money-making ideas, distractions, blessings, and quality people. (pg 76)

1. Recognition of _____. Explain. _____
_____
_____

2. Recognition of _____. Explain. _____
_____
_____

3. Recognition of _____. Explain. _____
_____
_____

4. Recognition of _____. Explain. _____
_____
_____

Part D: MONEY

> You are in a much better position to be able to increase the kingdom of God with money than without it. You have a right to be rich, but God is not going to entrust you with thousands of dollars if you have not been faithful with hundreds and He definitely will not entrust you with millions if you have not been faithful with thousands.

1. As I reflect back over my life, my financial situation has been:

___ pretty good   ___ pretty bad   ___ up and down   ___ I frequently struggle   ___ balanced

___ I sometimes struggle   ___ paycheck to paycheck   ___ I am pretty good with money

2. As you review the areas you have checked off, why do you think your financial situation has been the way it has been? _____
_____
_____

3. Would you consider yourself as financially responsible? ___yes ___no ___somewhat. Explain. _____
_____
_____

4. Do you consider yourself as a good steward over your money (tithing, paying bills on time, using money wisely)? ___yes   ___no ___somewhat. Explain. _____
_____
_____

5. If you are not consistent in paying your bills on time, then explain why this is. _____
_____
_____

6. Do you shop for unnecessary things when your bills are not paid (clothes, shoes, purses, jewelry, nails, etc.)
___yes ___no ___somewhat. Explain. _____
_____
_____

7. Are you consistent in paying your tithes (every time you get paid)? ___yes   ___no. Explain. _____
_____
_____

8. Would you like your financial situation to change? ___yes   ___no. Explain your answer. _____
_____
_____

9. Based on the things you have learned in this chapter and the things that prosperity is linked to, list some things you know you need to change in order for your financial situation to also change for the better?

    i. _____

    ii. _____

    iii. _____

    iv. _____

    v. _____

10. What date will you begin implementing these changes? _____

11. What date do you expect to see a MAJOR change in your finances? (ex. bills paid up, credit cards paid up, money in savings, etc. _____

> **Note to self:** If I have **NOT** been faithful with the little that God has entrusted me with, I cannot expect Him to bless me with more. I must first show myself responsible with what I already have.

Part E: PROSPERITY MINDSET

1. Do you think that you have a prosperity mindset? Explain _____
_____
_____

2. What is a prosperity mindset to you? _____

3. Have you ever had a unique idea that you thought would make you money and also help others? If yes, explain your ideas in as much detail as you can.

_____
_____
_____
_____
_____
_____
_____

3. What is stopping you from implementing that idea? _____
_____
_____

4. What is the greatest thing that could happen if you implemented this idea from beginning to end? _____
_____
_____
_____

5. How could your idea help others? _____
_____
_____
_____

6. What would it take right now for you to begin implementing your idea today? _____
_____
_____
_____

7. What are the first seven things that you could do to get started on the idea?

    i. _____

    ii. _____

    iii. _____

    iv. _____

    iv. _____

8. What date are you going to start on number one? _____

9. If you diligently worked on bringing this idea into fruition everyday, what realistic month/year do you think this idea can be realized? _____

10. What is stopping you from starting tomorrow (or today)? _____

_____

_____

_____

11. As you review your life, can you see any distractions that have prevented you from using your time more wisely or productively? If yes, explain. _____

12. Name a few things that you can see that may serve as distraction to you?

    i._____

    ii. _____

    iii._____

13. How are you going to change that?

_____

_____

_____

_____

Chapter 5: THE PROSPERITY CONSCIOUSNESS

On the lines below, journal about the main things that stuck with you from this chapter

Chapter 5 Answer Key

PART A: PROSPERITY

1. Based on what you have read, what is your definition of prosperity? **Answers may vary, but may include:**

> **Prosperity is a mindset. It may include health, wealth, peace, joy, success as well as money.**

2. Is it possible for someone to have inherited a million dollars and still not be prosperous? **Answers may vary, but may include:**

Yes, it is possible because prosperity is a mindset, therefore a person who has inherited a million dollars may spend the money recklessly because of their poverty mindset and may end up broke because their consciousness cannot hold on to the money.

3. Write a scripture from the bible that has to do with prosperity. Be sure to include the chapter and verse. **Answers may vary**
4. In your opinion, is it a sin to be rich? ___yes ___no; Explain. **There is no right or wrong answer.**
5. In your opinion, is it a sin to be poor? ___yes ___no; Explain. **There is no right or wrong answer.**
6. Is it possible to be cursed and rich? ___yes ___no; Explain. **There is no right or wrong answer.**
7. Is it possible to be poor and blessed? ___yes ___no; Explain. **There is no right or wrong answer.**

Part B: PROSPERITY LINKS

1. Prosperity is linked to my: **One of the following answers is fine.**

Self-discipline, Giving, Conversation, Friends, Gratitude, Actions, Recognition

Part C: RECOGNITION

Recognition of Recognition of Opportunities, Recognition of Money-making Ideas, Recognition of Quality people, Recognition of Distractions

Part D: MONEY

1. As I reflect back over my life, my financial situation has been: **Answers will vary.**
2. As you review the areas you have checked off, why do you think your financial situation has been the way it has been? **Answers will vary.**
3. Would you consider yourself as financially responsible? **Answers will vary.**
4. Do you consider yourself as a good steward over your money (tithing, paying bills on time, using money wisely)? **Answers will vary.**
5. If you are not consistent in paying your bills on time, then explain why this is. **Answers will vary.**
6. Do you shop for unnecessary things when your bills are not paid (clothes, shoes, purses, jewelry, nails, etc.)

Answers will vary.
7. Are you consistent in paying your tithes (every time you get paid)? ___yes   ___no. Explain. _____
Answers will vary.
8. Would you like your financial situation to change? ___yes   ___no. Explain your answer. _____
Answers will vary.
9. Based on the things you have learned in this chapter and the things that prosperity is linked to, list some things you know you need to change in order for your financial situation to also change for the better? **Answers will vary.**
10. What date will you begin implementing these changes? **Answers will vary.**
11. What date do you expect to see a MAJOR change in your finances? (ex. bills paid up, credit cards paid up, money in savings, etc. **Answers will vary.**

Part E: PROSPERITY MINDSET

1. Do you think that you have a prosperity mindset? Explain **Answers will vary.**
2. What is a prosperity mindset to you? **Answers will vary.**
3. Have you ever had a unique idea that you thought would make you money and also help others? If yes, explain your ideas in as much detail as you can. **Answers will vary.**
3. What is stopping you from implementing that idea? **Answers will vary.**
4. What is the greatest thing that could happen if you implemented this idea from beginning to end? **Answers will vary.**
5. How could your idea help others? **Answers will vary.**
6. What would it take right now for you to begin implementing your idea today? **Answers will vary.**
7. What are the first seven things that you could do to get started on the idea? **Answers will vary, but may include:**

- **Write a business plan**
- **Research information on my idea**
- **Make appointments with people who could give me valuable information**
- **Write down my idea in great detail**

8. What date are you going to start on number one? **Answers will vary.**
9. If you diligently worked on bringing this idea into fruition everyday, what realistic month/year do you think this idea can be realized? **Answers will vary.**
10. What is stopping you from starting tomorrow (or today)? **Answers will vary.**
11. As you review your life, can you see any distractions that have prevented you from using your time more wisely or productively? If yes, explain. **Answers will vary.**
12. Name a few things that you can see that may serve as distraction to you? **Answers will vary, but may include:**

**Children, Household choirs, Watch television too much
Gossip, Telephone, Wasting time**

13. How are you going to change that? **Answers will vary.**

Chapter 6
Amazing Grace

God's grace is available to everyone, including the unsaved. *"For the grace of God that brings salvation hath appeared to all men" (Titus 2:11).* Christ did the work to make salvation available to all.

EXCERPTS

◆ God gave His Word as a revelation of Himself. Every new truth discerned is a fresh disclosure of the character of God. Both witnesses, the old and the New Testament point to the plan of salvation.

◆ When God's children neglect to search the scriptures for themselves, they are led to accept false interpretations and cherish doctrines which have no foundation in the Bible.

◆ The scriptures give transforming, educating, power that expands the mind, sharpens the perceptions and ripens the judgment. It gives stability of purpose, patience, courage and fortitude; it refines your character and sanctifies your soul.

◆ The Word of God is true from beginning to end. It will come to pass if God spoke it. Even if the promise has been delayed, it will not be denied.

◆ It moves the heart of God when we bring Him in remembrance of His Word.

Chapter 6 Activity

PART A: FREE-WILL & SELF CHOICE

> We must always keep in mind that God gives us free will and self choice. God never forces the will or the conscience, but He does give warnings first. He never just sits and allows us to make mistakes.

1. According to what you have learned, what is grace? _____
_____

2. What does it mean that God has given us "free-well" and "self-choice"? _____
_____
_____

3. How does God give us warnings before we make the wrong decisions? In other words, through what avenues can He warn us? _____
_____
_____

4. Name some emotions you have experienced in order to make you the unique person you are today?
_____
_____

5. What does the phrase, *"In much wisdom is much grief; He that increases understanding increases sorrow (Ecclesiastes 1:18)"* mean? How can having wisdom and discernment be discouraging? _____
_____
_____

6. What does "emotional baggage" mean? _____
_____
_____

7. There are some things that have happened to you that have changed you temporarily and other things that may have scared you permanently. Did something happen to you that scared you permanently? _____

8. If yes, what was it? _____
_____
_____
_____

9. How did the above situation change the way you see people and situations? _____

10. Would you consider the feelings you have from the situation to be "Emotional Baggage?" _____

11. Do you think this situation affects your relationships with other people? If yes, explain. _____
_____
_____

12. Is someone else involved in this situation that you need to forgive? _____

13. Are you willing to forgive? If yes, pretend as though the person is in front of you. Write down what you will say to them to express your forgiveness. _____
_____
_____
_____

14. Now review the words you wrote. Do they indicate true forgiveness or is there hidden bitterness or anger? If there is some hidden bitterness and/or anger in your words, then try again on the lines below.
_____
_____
_____

15. What other ways can you begin to release any emotional baggage that you may have?

    i._____

    ii_____

    iii_____

    iv_____

    v_____

PART B: UNFORGIVENESS

> The inability to forgive has been the most widespread sin that blocks a deliverance from occurring. Unforgiveness is one of the primary tools that Satan uses to gain a stronghold into a believer's life. It is a stronghold, having a very "strong" "hold" on a person. (pg. 952)

1. Name three benefits that forgiving others does for the one forgiving.

    i._____

    ii_____

    iii_____

2. Explain how you can forgive someone without them being there. _____

_____

_____

3. How can unforgiveness be detrimental for the one who refuses to forgive? _____

_____

_____

_____

NOTE: If it is still hard for you to forgive someone for something done to you, know that the longer you choose not to forgive, the longer you, yourself will be in bondage. Unforgiveness keeps you captive and prevents you from walking into the higher things of God.

4. What do you think it will take for you to be able to forgive everyone who hurt you? _____
_____
_____
_____

5. Are you willing to try the steps necessary that will get you closer to forgiveness? _____

If you answered YES, then that's a GREAT start!

PART C: HUMILITY

> Humility comes before exaltation. *Humble yourselves under the mighty Hand of God, that He may exalt you in due time.*
> *(1 Peter 5:6).*

1. Why is having humility better than having pride? _____
_____
_____

2. What have we learned about how God views humility? _____
_____

3. Why is having humility a good thing? _____

_____

_____

4. Humility leads the people of God into worship. Fill in the correct word next to its proper definition.

Thanking God for what He has done for us by singing, dancing, shouting and playing musical instruments is _____.

In solemn humility, with an open heart and bowed spirit, we honor Him just because of who He is, is called _____.

PART D: THE POWER OF PRAYER

> From the secret places of prayer come powers that shake the world. Your prayer life should be a continuous, daily and automatic practice. Prayer should be as automatic as brushing your teeth. (pg 98)

1. What do angels ascending Jacob's ladder signify? _____

_____

_____

2. What do angels descending signify? _____

_____

_____

3. According to what we have learned How can a prayer be delayed from manifesting on the earth? _____

_____

_____

4. What does it mean to enter spiritual warfare? _____

_____

_____

5. What does Satan try and make us think about our prayers when they are not answered in the timeframe we think they should be answered? _____

_____

_____

6. In order to enter spiritual warfare, we must be equipped with what? _____

_____

_____

7. What can happen if you enter spiritual warfare without being known in the spirit realm? _____

_____

_____

8. Why is it important to know the scriptures, be equipped with the armor of God and be bold when entering spiritual warfare? _____

_____

_____

9. On the lines below, name **two** scriptures that you know by heart. These scriptures can help you when you are in spiritual warfare.

    i. _____

_____

    ii. _____

_____

PART D: GRATITUDE

On the lines below, list the reasons that you have to be grateful.

1. _____
2. _____
3. _____
4. _____
5. _____
6. _____
7. _____
8. _____
9. _____
10. _____
11. _____
12. _____
13. _____
14. _____

> Gratitude unlocks the fullness of life. It turns what we have into enough & more. It turns denial into acceptance, chaos to order confusion to clarity. It can turn a meal into a feast, a house into a home, a stranger into a friend. Gratitude makes sense of our past and brings peace for today, & creates a vision for tomorrow.
> ~Dr. Mia Y. Merritt

Chapter 6: AMAZING GRACE

On the lines below, journal about the main things that stuck with you from this chapter

Chapter 6 Answer Key

PART A: FREE-WILL & SELF CHOICE

1. According to what you have learned, what is grace? **Answers will vary, but may include:**
   Grace is a priceless gift from God. It is the Father's love towards us, even though we do not deserve it.

2. What does it mean that God has given us "free-well" and "self-choice"? **Answers will vary, but may include:**

   Self-choice means that God allows people to make their own decisions. He does not force us to choose rightly, but He does give us warnings and nudges

   Free-will means that are able to behave, speak and act as we will. He does not force us to do right, but he does give us warnings to do right.

3. How does God give us warnings before making the wrong decisions? In other words, through what avenues can warn us? **Answers will vary, but may include:**

   He speaks to us by the most convenient avenue to us. This may include people via strangers, family, friends, the preacher, ministers, TV, radio, books, magazines, newspapers, etc.

4. What are some of the emotions we have gone through in order to make us the unique person we are today? **Answers will vary, but may include:**

   Happiness, sadness, grief, anger, unforgiveness, bitterness, excitement, triumph, defeat, depression, success, prosperity failure, etc.

5. What does the phrase, *"In much wisdom is much grief. He that increases understanding increases sorrow (Ecclesiastes 1:18)"* mean? How can having wisdom and discernment be a bad thing? **Answers will vary, but may include:**

   This means that as you grow in wisdom and discernment, you begin to see things with the spiritual eye that are disheartening, hurtful and could be discouraging.

6. What is "emotional baggage" to you? **Answers will vary, but may include:**
   Emotional Baggage is comprised of all the emotions and feelings that developed from those negative, painful or shameful events that happened in the past.

7. There are some things that have happened to you that have changed you temporarily and other things that may have scared you permanently. Did something happen to you that scared you permanently? **Answers will vary**
8. What was it? **Answers will vary.**
9. How did the above situation change the way you see people and situations? **Answers will vary.**

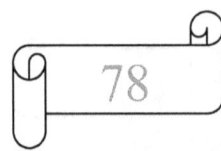

10. Would you consider the feelings you have from the situation to be "Emotional Baggage?" **Answers will vary.**
11. Do you think this situation affects your relationships with other people. If yes, explain. **Answers will vary.**
12. Is someone else involved in this situation that you need to forgive? **Answers will vary.**
13. Are you willing to forgive? If yes, pretend as though the person is face to face with you. Write down exactly how you will express your forgiveness to them. **Answers will vary.**
14. Now review the words you wrote. Are they indicative of true forgiveness or is there some hidden bitterness. If there is some hidden bitterness and anger in your words, then try again on the lines below. **Answers will vary.**
15. What other ways can you begin to release any emotional baggage that you may have? **Answers will vary, but may include:**

PART B: UNFORGIVENESS

1. Name three benefits that forgiving others does for the one forgiving. **Answers will vary, but may include:**

- **Forgiving others frees you from bondage**
- **It releases a burden from your soul**
- **It decreases your chances of getting sick**
- **It sets you free.**

2. Explain how you can forgive someone without them being there. **Answers will vary, but may include:**

> **Forgiveness is a decision to simply let it go. Once you confess your unforgiveness to God, you can release the hurt or betrayal out of your soul and refuse to pick it up again. The person who hurt you does not have to be there.**

3. How can unforgiveness be detrimental for the one who refuses to forgive? **Answers will vary, but may include:**

- **It is a heavy burden**
- **It causes sickness**
- **It makes you bitter, angry and negative**
- **It keeps you in bondage**

NOTE: If it is still hard for you to forgive someone for something done to you, know that the longer you choose not to forgive, the longer you, yourself will be in bondage. Unforgivness keeps you captive and prevents you from walking into the higher things of God.

4. What do you think it will take for you to be able to forgive everyone who hurt you? **Answers will vary, but may include:**
5. Are you willing to try the steps necessary that will get you closer to forgiveness? **Answers will vary.**

PART C: HUMILITY

1. Why is having humility better than having pride? **Answers will vary, but may include:**
- **God gives grace the humble**

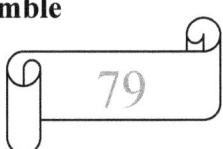

- We move the heart of God when we are humble
- Before humility is exaltation
- God has called us to be humble servants before Him

2. What have we learned about how God views humility? **Answers will vary, but may include: His judgment or punishment can be delayed or postponed when we humble ourselves. It touches His heart when we humble ourselves before Him.**

3. Why is having humility a good thing? **Answers will vary, but may include:**
We may get God's favor by being humble
Humility comes before exaltation

4. Humility leads the people of God into worship. Fill in the correct word next to its proper definition.

Thanking God for what He has done for us by singing, dancing, shouting and playing musical instruments is **PRAISE**

In solemn humility, with an open heart and bowed spirit, we honor Him just because of who He is, is called **WORSHIP**

PART D: THE POWER OF PRAYER

1. What do angels ascending Jacob's ladder signify? **Angels ascending on Jacob's ladder signifies the heavenly beings taking the prayers of believers up to God.**

2. What do angels descending signify? **Angels descending on Jacob's ladder signifies the heavenly beings brining the answered prayers, solutions to problems or blessings down to earth to the people of God.**

3. How can a prayer be delayed from manifesting on the earth according to what we have learned? **Answers may vary, but may include the fact that principalities, powers, evil forces and ungodly spirits are always trying to intercept the prayers from going up and the blessings from coming down.**

4. What does it mean to enter spiritual warfare? Entering spiritual warfare means entering the spiritual realm with the armor of God, speaking directly to **principalities, powers, evil forces and ungodly spirits by using the word of God and speaking directly to them with the blood and power of Jesus.**

5. What does Satan try and make us think about our prayers when they are not answered in the timeframe we think they should be answered? **He wants us to think that our prayers are not being heard by God and that we are just wasting our time praying, but that is a LIE!**

6. In order to enter spiritual warfare, we must be equipped with what? **Before you enter spiritual warfare, you must be sure that you are properly equipped with the Word of God, that you are effectively prayed up, that you have a consistent prayer life and that you are known in the spirit world.**

7. What can happen if you enter spiritual warfare without being known in the spirit realm? **If you are not properly equipped spiritually, you can become overcome by the evil spirits in the dark world and can even have a demon transferred to you.**

8. Why is it important to know the scriptures, be equipped with the right armor and be bold when entering spiritual warfare? **Because knowing the scriptures builds you up in the most holy faith, it is the proper way we are to respond to Satan and his evil spirits, the armor of God is real in the spirit world and allows you to stand against the fiery darts of the enemy.**

On the lines below, write four scriptures that you know by heart.

PART D: GRATITUDE

On the lines below, list the reasons that you have to be grateful. **Answers will vary.**

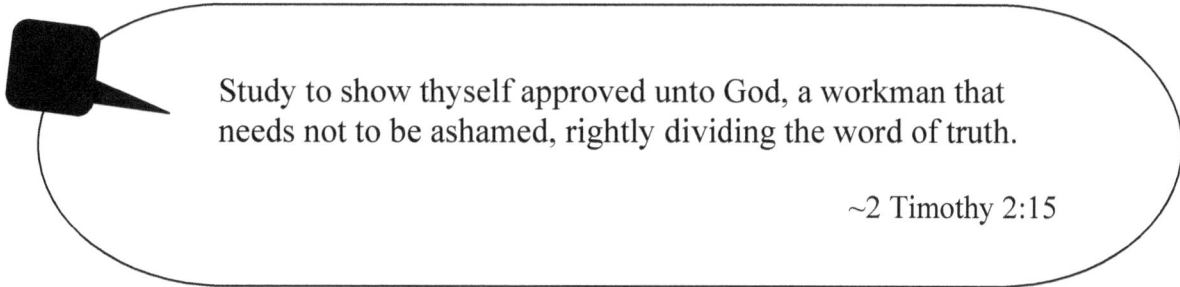

Study to show thyself approved unto God, a workman that needs not to be ashamed, rightly dividing the word of truth.

~2 Timothy 2:15

Chapter 7
Holding on to His Promises

So shall my Word be that goeth forth out of my mouth: it shall not return unto me void, but it shall accomplish that which I please, and it shall prosper in the thing whereto I sent it.
(Isaiah 55:11-12)

EXCERPTS

- God gave His Word as a revelation of Himself. Every new truth discerned is a fresh disclosure of the character of God. Both witnesses, the old and the New Testament point to the plan of salvation.

- When God's children neglect to search the scriptures for themselves, they are led to accept false interpretations and cherish doctrines which have no foundation in the Bible.

- The scriptures give transforming, educating, power that expands the mind, sharpens the perceptions and ripens the judgment. It gives stability of purpose, patience, courage and fortitude; it refines your character and sanctifies your soul.

- The Word of God is true from beginning to end. It will come to pass if God spoke it. Even if the promise has been delayed, it will not be denied.

- It moves the heart of God when we bring Him in remembrance of His Word.

PART A: THE SACRED SCRIPTURES

> We must always keep in mind that God gives us free will and self choice. God never forces the will or the conscience, but He does give warnings first. He never just sits and allows us to make mistakes.

1. Based upon what you have read, why is it that many people do not know who they are in God?

   _____

   _____

2. What is one sure way of discovering who you are in God and finding out what His will is for your life?

   _____

   _____

3. Based upon what you have learned, why did God ask Adam where he was? _____

   _____

   _____

4. Both the Old and the New Testament are relevant to the plan of salvation. How does the Old Testament relate to the plan of salvation? _____

   _____

   _____

5. How does the New Testament relate to the plan of salvation? _____

   _____

   _____

6. Are we supposed to disregard the Old Testament now that we have the New Testament? Explain.

   _____

   _____

PART B: BRING HIM IN REMEMBRANCE

> When you pray His Word back to Him, that gets His attention! Learn to give God His Word back to Him. He encourages us to do that. In fact, in Isaiah 43:26, He says, *Put me in remembrance.* Bring back to God what He has said about you.

1. Why is it important to have the Word of God on this inside of you? _____
_____
_____

2. What does God mean when he says in Isaiah 43:26, "*Put me in remembrance*"? _____
_____
_____

3. Why does Satan want to keep the people of God out of the Word of God? _____
_____
_____

4. What does the Word of God do for the person who meditates upon it frequently? _____
_____
_____

5. What is your favorite Bible Verse: Book: _____ chapter _____ Verse: _____ Scripture: _____
_____
_____

6. Why do you like that scripture so much? _____
_____
_____

PART C: LEARNING THE SCRIPTURES

On the lines below, write down <u>five</u> scriptures that you do not yet know by memory, but will make a commitment to learn.

    i. Book: _____ chapter _____ Verse: _____

_____

_____

    Start date: _____ **Date Learned:** _____

    ii. Book: _____ chapter _____ Verse: _____

_____

_____

    Start date: _____ **Date Learned:** _____

    iii. Book: _____ chapter _____ Verse: _____

_____

_____

    Start date: _____ **Date Learned:** _____

    iv. Book: _____ chapter _____ Verse: _____

_____

_____

    Start date: _____ **Date Learned:** _____

    v. Book: _____ chapter _____ Verse: _____

_____

_____

    Start date: _____ **Date Learned:** _____

> **Note to self:** The word of God will expand my mind, sharpen my perception, ripen my judgment and sanctify my soul!

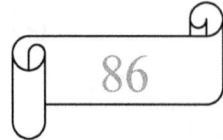

PART D: THE SECRET PLACE

1. How often do you pray? _____
_____

2. Do you have a designated, blocked-out time with God? _____

3. If not, how and when do you pray (check all that apply)? _____

____everyday   ____several times a day   ____about 3 times a week   ____at least once a week

____on Sundays   ____ I pray in my mind often   ____a few times a month   ____I don't pray

4. Explain how and when you usually talk to God. _____

5. As you review what you have checked off above, are you satisfied with how often you pray? _____

6. If no, are you willing to change it? _____

7. If yes, how will you change it? _____
_____

8. What date are you willing to start? _____

9. How do you think increasing your time with God in prayer will change you? _____
_____

10. Chapter eight talked about the "Secret Place". Do you have a secret place that you meet God? _____

11. If not, would you like to have one? _____

12. Where in your house would be a good place to meet God where you can be undisturbed and uninterrupted in order to hear from Him? _____
_____

The effectual fervent prayer of a righteous man avails much! (James 5:16)

Chapter 7: HOLDING ON TO HIS PROMISES

On the lines below, journal about the main things that stuck with you from this chapter

Chapter 7 Answer Key

PART A: THE SACRED SCRIPTURES

> We must always keep in mind that God gives us free will and self choice. God never forces the will or the conscience, but He does give warnings first. He never just sits and allows us to make mistakes.

1. Based upon what you have read, why is it that many people do not know who they are in God?

    Many people do not know who they are in God because they do not study His Word enough to find out His will for their life.

2. What is one sure way of discovering who you are in God and finding out what His will for your life is?
    Prayer and the study of God's sacred Word.

3. Based upon what you have learned, why did God ask Adam where he was?
    Because Adam himself did not know where He was anymore in relation to God. When God asked him, *"Where are you?"* God was not talking about a place or space, He was talking about identity. God knew where Adam was both in the natural and in the Spirit, but He needed Adam to recognize this.

4. Both the Old and the New Testament are relevant to the plan of salvation. How does the Old Testament relate to the plan of salvation? **The types, sacrifices and prophecies of the Old Testament point to the Savior to come.**

5. How does the New Testament relate to the plan of salvation? **The gospels and epistles of the New Testament tell of a Savior who has already come in the exact manner foretold by prophecy.**

6. Are we supposed to disregard the Old Testament now that we have the New Testament? Explain. **No, because very inspired Word in both the Old and New Testament is relevant, pertinent and applicable.**

PART B: BRING HIM IN REMEMBRANCE

1. Why is it important to have the Word of God on this inside of you? **Because there will come a time or a situation where you will need the word of God and a physical Bible will not be handy. You will have to pull out what's on the inside of you in order to get a breakthrough in a particular situation.**

2. What does God mean when he says in Isaiah 43:26, *"Put me in remembrance"*? **God is telling us that it is okay to remind Him of the promises that He has spoken over our lives. This is not because He forgets, but it shows Him that we know His Word and we have faith that He will accomplish what He has spoken.**

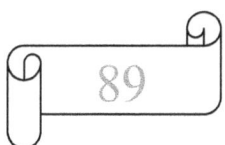

3. What does Satan want to keep the people of God out of the Word of God? **Satan knows that the people of God get their strength from the Word of God and prayer. There is educating transforming power in the word of God that expands the mind, sharpens the judgment and ripens the perceptions. The word of God refines the character, sanctifies the soul and gives us revelation concerning God's plan for our lives.**

4. What does the Word of God do for the person who meditates upon it frequently? It **expands the mind, sharpens the judgment and ripens the perceptions. The word of God refines the character, sanctifies the soul and gives us revelation concerning God's plan for our lives.**

5. What is your favorite Bible Verse: Book: **Answers will vary**

6. Why do you like that scripture so much? **Answers will vary**

PART C: LEARNING THE SCRIPTURES

On the lines below, write down <u>five</u> scriptures that you do not yet know my memory, but will make a commitment to learn them. **Answers will vary**

PART D: THE SECRET PLACE

1. How often do you pray? **Answers will vary**
2. Do you have a designated, blocked-out time with God? **Answers will vary**
3. If not, how and when do you pray (check all that apply)? **Answers will vary**
4. Explain how and when you usually talk to God. **Answers will vary**
5. As you review what you have checked off above, are you satisfied with how often you pray? **Answers will vary**
6. If no, are you willing to change it? **Answers will vary**
7. If yes, how will you change it? **Answers will vary**
8. What date are you willing to start? **Answers will vary**
9. How do you think increasing your time with God in prayer will change you? **Answers will vary**
10. Chapter eight talked about the "Secret Place". Do you have a secret place that you meet God? **Answers will vary**
11. If not, would you like to have one? **Answers will vary**
12. Where in your house would be a good place to meet God where you can be undisturbed and uninterrupted in order to hear from Him? **Answers will vary**

Chapter 8
Victory in Christ!

But thanks be to God, which gives us the victory through our Lord Jesus Christ.

1 Corinthians 15:57

- ◆ Sometimes our own words and behaviors can cause problems for us. We often blame the devil for certain hell that breaks loose in our lives, but there are times when Satan has nothing to do with the problems we experience. He just takes the credit and has no problem doing so.

- ◆ You attract what you talk about. When you change your belief system in thought, words, and emotional pattern, you change your whole body, you change your situations and you change your reality.

- ◆ If your thoughts are negative, you will exude a negative disposition and the words that you speak will be negative, thus attracting negativity to you. If your thoughts are positive, then your conversation will be of a positive nature, thus attracting good to you.

- ◆ There is a veil that separates the spiritual world from the natural world. We, as carnal beings see with the natural eyes, but at times, we see with the eyes of the heart with spiritual vision. It is during these times that God gives us glimpses of our marvelous future.

- ◆ A Book of Remembrance is written before God, in which are recorded the good deeds of *"them that feared the Lord and that thought upon His name"* *Malachi 3:16.*

PART A: POWER

> When we are enlightened by the power that is available to us, in us, and in the sacred scriptures, we become elevated and authoritative in the spirit.

1. How do we have Victory in Christ Jesus? _____
_____
_____

2. As we grow in wisdom, what kinds of things does wisdom reveal to us? _____
_____
_____

3. Name three things that you have learned about the "**Armor of God**". _____

    i. _____

    ii. _____

    iii. _____

4. Name three things that you have learned about the "Power of the **Holy Spirit**". _____

    i. _____

    ii. _____

    iii. _____

5. Name three things that you have learned about "**Spiritual Gifts**".

    i. _____

    ii. _____

    iii. _____

6. Name three things that you have learned about the "**Power of Your Tongue**".

    i._____

    ii._____

    iii._____

7. Name three things that you have learned about the "**Power of the Mind**".

    i._____

    ii._____

    iii._____

8. Name three things that you have learned about the "**Power of Self-confidence**".

    i._____

    ii._____

    iii._____

9. How do you feel about the popular saying, "Once saved always saved." Do you believe the statement to be true? Explain. _____

_____

_____

_____

_____

PART B: RULES OF ENGAGMENT

1. What have you learned about "The Sanctuary"? _____

_____

_____

_____

2. What was the purpose of the "Sin Offering"? _____

3. Explain what the Priest did on the "Day of Atonement". _____+_____

_____

_____

_____

4. Why were the sins of the people transferred to an innocent animal? _____

_____

_____

5. Why did this practice symbolize? _____

_____

_____

6. Whose going to suffer the final punishment for the sins of all people? _____

_____

_____

7. Who did the priest represent in their role in carrying out the various offerings brought by the people?

_____

_____

8. After the Jews rejected their Savoir and Redeemer, how did that affect their offerings?

_____

_____

9. Why do we no longer sacrifice animals to atone for sin? _____

_____

_____

PART C: THE BOOKS

1. What does it mean to have spiritual vision? _____
_____
_____

2. Explain in your own words what the BOOK OF REMEMBRANCE is: _____
_____
_____

3. Explain in your own words what the BOOK OF RECORD is: _____
_____
_____

4. Explain in your own words what the BOOK OF LIFE is: _____

5. What does the scripture, "I will NOT blot out his name out of the book of life" (Rev 3:5) mean?
_____
_____

6. Why is it a blessing to be able to overcome? _____
_____
_____

PART D: THE OVERCOMERS

1. Name at least five blessings that Jesus has promised to the over comers.

    i. _____
    ii. _____
    iii. _____
    iv. _____

iv. _____

Chapter 8: VICTORY IN CHRIST

On the lines below, journal about the main things that stuck with you from this chapter

Chapter 8 Answer Key

PART A: POWER

1. How do we have Victory in Christ Jesus? **We have victory in Christ through prayer, perseverance, reading the Bible, spiritual warfare, having faith and trusting in Him.**

2. As we grow in wisdom, what kinds of things does wisdom reveal to us? **Wisdom reveals our purpose in God, the treasures of truth found in the word of God, hidden things about ourselves and gives us discernment.**

3. Name three things that you have learned about the "Armor of God". Answers may vary, but may include,

   - While we do not see the armor in the natural, it is real in the spirit world.
   - This Armor is absolutely necessary in order to counteract spiritual attacks.
   - When we clothe ourselves with the armor, we step out fully equipped to quench all the fiery darts shot at us by spiritual enemies.

4. Name three things that you have learned about the "Power of the Holy Spirit". Answers may vary, but may include,

   - The Holy Spirit is the Third Person of the Godhead, coequal with the Father and the Son.
   - We receive the indwelling of the Holy Spirit the moment we receive Jesus Christ as our Lord and Savior.
   - Jesus sent us this precious gift as a replacement for His absence.
   - The Father, the Son, and the Holy Spirit are one in power, but distinct in their functions
   - The Holy Spirit does the work that Jesus did when He was on earth.
   - The Holy Spirit takes up permanent residence in the hearts of believers and is the revealer of truth.
   - There are many functions of the Holy Spirit, but the main functions are to guide believers into all truth (John 16:13); testify of Jesus (John 15:26); produce His fruit in our lives (Galatians 5:22); and impart believers with spiritual gifts (1 Corinthians 12).

5. Name three things that you have learned about "Spiritual Gifts". Answers may vary, but may include,

   - Spiritual gifts significantly assist believers in their Christian walk.
   - The power of Spirit-given gifts aids believers in prayer, in spiritual warfare, in edifying the body of Christ, in refreshing the soul, in confusing the enemy and in building up the kingdom of God.
   - While there are different kinds of gifts, spiritual gifts are God-given graces meant for works of service to benefit and build up the body of Christ as a whole.

6. Name three things that you have learned about the "**Power of Your Tongue**". **Answers may vary, but may include,**

- **Words are thoughts and are an invisible power that will finally objectify in the form they are given.**
- **Your words can magnetize prosperity, harmony, peace, and good toward you or draw trouble, poverty, discord, frustration and evil toward you.**
- **The more specific you are when speaking positive, the quicker the manifestation, the greater you feel, the more powerful the materialization.**
- **Definite statements produce definite results. Feeling is essential in order for words to manifest.**

7. Name three things that you have learned about the "**Power of the Mind**". **Answers may vary, but may include,**

- **The thoughts you think are magnets. They attract things to you.**
- **The thoughts that you entertain determines your mental attitude.**
- **Your thoughts which lead to your attitude influence people for or against you**
- **Every one of your daily secret thoughts are real things, which are acting on the thoughts of other people.**
- **A positive attitude is your lottery ticket that will win for you in every situation!**

8. Name three things that you have learned about the "**Power of Self-confidence**". **Answers may vary, but may include,**

- **Those who truly know their Lord are some of the most self-confident people are on earth.**
- **With self-confidence in knowing your God and having the assurance that He knows you, the appearances of problems in the natural do not shake your faith because you stand upon a solid Rock.**
- **Having self-confidence in knowing who you are gives you boldness is saying what God has instructed you to say.**
- **Confidence is necessary if you are to teach, preach, evangelize or minister.**
- **You must know that you know your Lord and believe on His name if you are to persuade anyone else to know that they know and believe on His name.**

9. How do you feel about the popular saying, "Once saved always saved." Do you believe the statement to be true? Explain. **Answers may vary, but may include,**

If a person could not lose their salvation, Jesus would not have written that their names could be BLOTTED out of the Book of Life.

PART B: RULES OF ENGAGMENT

1. What have you learned about "The Sanctuary"? **Answers may vary, but may include,**

- The term "sanctuary" in the Bible, refers to the tabernacle built by Moses.
- The sanctuary in heaven, where Jesus now ministers on our behalf is the great original.
- The sanctuary built by Moses was a copy of what is in heaven.
- The earthly sanctuary was a figure for the time then present, in which were offered both gifts and sacrifices.
- Upon this altar were consumed all the sacrifices offered to the Lord and consumed by fire from the Lord

2. What was the purpose of the "Sin Offering"?

The sin offering provided forgiveness, while the other goat provided the removal of sin. The high priest, having taken an offering for the congregation, went into the Holy of Holies with the blood from the first goat and sprinkled it upon the mercy seat, above the tables of the Law.

3. Explain what the Priest did on the "Day of Atonement".

On the Day of Atonement, the high priest was to take two male goats for a sin offering. One goat was sacrificed as a sin offering for the people of Israel (Leviticus 16:15), while the other goat was released into the wilderness to be the scapegoat (Leviticus 16:20-22).

4. Why were the sins of the people transferred to an innocent animal?

The sins of the people were transferred to the animal and he became a substitute and a sacrifice for the sins of the people. He received the penalty of sin that the sinner should have received.

5. Why did this practice symbolize?

This symbolized the perfect offering of Jesus Christ. Through the blood of this victim, man looked forward by faith to the blood of Christ which would atone for the sins of the world. *"Without the shedding of blood there is no forgiveness" (Hebrews 9:22).*

6. Whose going to suffer the final punishment for the sins of all people?

Since Satan is the originator of sin and the direct instigator of all sins, justice demands that he suffer the final punishment.

7. Who did the priest represent in their role in carrying out the various offerings brought by the people?

The priesthood was established to represent the character and work of Christ.

8. After the Jews rejected their Savoir and Redeemer, how did that affect their offerings?

Him to death, they rejected all that gave significance to the temple and its services. Its sacredness had departed. From that day, the sacrificial offerings and the services connected with them were meaningless. They were left in total darkness to continue their futile sacrifices and offerings.

9. Why do we no longer sacrifice animals to atone for sin?

Animal sacrifices came to an end with Jesus Christ, the precious Lamb that was slain. Jesus Christ was the ultimate and final sacrificial substitute (Hebrews 7:27) and is now the only mediator between God and humanity (1 Timothy 2:5).

PART C: THE BOOKS

1. What does it mean to have spiritual vision? **Answers may vary, but may include:**

Spiritual vision means to be able to look pass the natural and be able to see things the way they are in the realm of the spirit. This may include discernment, open visions, impressions, dreams, or having the Words of the scriptures open up to you as you are studying them.

2. Explain in your own words what the BOOK OF REMEMBRANCE is:
In this book, every deed of righteousness is immortalized. There, every temptation resisted, every evil overcome, every word of tender pity expressed, every act of sacrifice, every suffering and sorrow endured for Christ's sake, is recorded and faithfully chronicled in this book.

3. Explain in your own words what the BOOK OF RECORD is:
This book is being updated every day. As the Books of Record are opened in the judgment, the lives of all who have believed on Jesus come in review before God. If any have sins written on the books of record that have not been repented of, their names will be blotted out of the Book of Life, and the record of their good deeds will be erased from the book of God's remembrance.

4. Explain in your own words what the BOOK OF LIFE is: **Answers may vary, but may include**
This book is similar to the Book of Remembrance in which are recorded the deeds of those who have feared (reverenced) the Lord and walked in His ways. The same book is also called the Lamb's Book of Life because it contains the names of those who have been redeemed by the blood of the Lord Jesus.

5. What does the scripture, "I will NOT blot out his name out of the book of life" (Rev 3:5) mean? **Answers may vary, but may include,**
If a person could not lose their salvation, Jesus would not have written that their names could be BLOTTED out of the Book of Life.

6. Why is it a blessing to be able to overcome? **Answers may vary, but may include, the fact that Jesus has many blessings waiting for those who overcome.**

PART D: THE OVERCOMERS

1. Name at least five blessings that Jesus has promised to the over comers. **Answers may include:**

- *He that overcomes shall not be hurt of the second death (Revelation 2:11).*
- *To him that overcomes will I give to eat of the hidden manna, and will give him a white stone, and in the stone a new name written, which no man knows except he that receives it (Revelation 2:17).*
- *And he that overcomes, and keeps my works unto the end, to him will I give power over the nations (Revelation 2:26).*
- *He that overcomes, the same shall be clothed in white raiment; and I will not blot out his name out of the book of life, but I will confess his name before my Father, and before His angels (Revelation 3:5).*
- *To him that overcomes will I grant to sit with me in my throne even as I also overcame and am sat down with my father in His throne (Revelation 3:21).*

Dr. Mia Y. Merritt

www.miamerritt.com
merrittmia@yahoo.com
1-866-560-7652

Dr. Mia Y. Merritt was born and raised in Miami Florida and matriculated in the Miami-Dade County Public School System. She is an educator with over 17 years experience working as a teacher, Assistant Principal, College Professor and mentor. She is a Certified Keynote Speaker, Teen/Youth Facilitator, Prosperity Coach and Author.

Dr. Merritt has provided workshops, seminars and keynote speeches around the country to organizations such as the U.S. Department of Homeland Security, The Miami-Dade County City Mangers, FIU Executive Staff, University of Miami Public Relations Department, Family Christian Association and many more.

She is also a Minister of the Gospel and is a member of Peace Missionary Baptist Church in Miami, Florida under the leadership of Rev. Dr. Tracy McCloud. Dr. Merritt is the recipient of the 2011 African American Achiever's Award sponsored by JM Family Enterprises.

She holds a Bachelors Degree in Elementary Education, a Masters Degree in Exceptional Education, a Specialist Degree in Educational Leadership and a Doctorate Degree in Organizational Leadership.

Dr. Merritt is a published author of eight books on the subjects of spirituality, personal development, prosperity, self-empowerment, and adult education. Her books focus on living in peace with oneself and others by making right choices and understanding cause and effect. He books focus on living with integrity and serving others. Dr. Merritt's challenges and experiences in life have produced in her the resilience, character and strength to persevere in spite of what challenges she face. She shares her experiences in order to inspire, encourage and remind that your past does not dictate your future.

Her favorite Bible Scripture comes from Jeremiah 29:11: *For I know the thoughts that I think toward you, saith the Lord, thoughts of peace, and not of evil, to give you an expected end. Then shall ye call upon me, and ye shall go and pray unto me, and I will hearken unto you. And ye shall seek me, and find me, when ye shall search for me with all your heart. And I will be found of you, saith the Lord.*

www.ingramcontent.com/pod-product-compliance
Lightning Source LLC
Chambersburg PA
CBHW081258170426
43198CB00017B/2831